Church Catholic

**Little Manual of the Sacred Heart**

Enlarged Edition

Church Catholic

**Little Manual of the Sacred Heart**
*Enlarged Edition*

ISBN/EAN: 9783337300272

Printed in Europe, USA, Canada, Australia, Japan

Cover: Foto ©Lupo / pixelio.de

More available books at **www.hansebooks.com**

# "Son, Give Me Thy Heart."

"The amiable Heart of Jesus has an infinite desire to be known and loved by its creatures, in which it wishes to establish its reign, as the source of every good, in order to provide for all their wants."

(*Blessed Margaret Mary.*)

# LITTLE MANUAL

OF THE

# SACRED HEART.

A COLLECTION OF

INSTRUCTIONS, PRAYERS, HYMNS,

AND VARIOUS PRACTICES OF PIETY,

IN HONOR OF THE

## SACRED HEART OF JESUS.

*Enlarged Edition.*

"I will speak to his heart and from it obtain whatever I shall desire."—ST. BONAVENTURE.

NEW YORK:
J. SCHAEFER, PUBLISHER,
60 Barclay Street.

1887,

IMPRIMATUR,

✠ JOHN CARDINAL MC CLOSKEY,
Archbishop of New York.

COPYRIGHTED
BY
JOSEPH SCHAEFER.

1885.

A. M. D. G.

TO THE

MERCIFULLY LOVING AND THRICE HOLY

HEART OF JESUS,

TO WHOM BE HONOR & GLORY FOR EVER & EVER,

THIS

MANUAL OF THE SACRED HEART

IS

WITH DEEPEST GRATITUDE AND BOUNDLESS CONFIDENCE,

HUMBLY DEDICATED.

# CONTENTS.

| | PAGE |
|---|---|
| Introduction | iii |
| Promises of Our Lord to Blessed Margaret Mary | 10 |
| Act of Consecration to the Sacred Heart | 11 |
| The Little Chaplet of the Sacred Heart | 12 |
| The Litany of the Sacred Heart | 18 |
| Ejaculation | 21 |
| Guard of Honor of the Sacred Heart | 22 |
| Office of the Sacred Heart | 29 |
| Dwelling in the Sacred Heart | 37 |
| Prayer to the Sacred Heart | 42 |
| Ejaculation | 43 |
| Hymn to Jesus | 44 |
| Visit to a picture of the Sacred Heart | 45 |
| Feast of the Sacred Heart | 45 |
| Month of the Sacred Heart | 45 |
| Novena in Honor of the Sacred Heart | 46 |
| A Devout Aspiration to the Sacred Heart | 51 |
| Rosary of the Sacred Heart | 52 |
| Act of Consecration to the Sacred Heart, approved by the Congregation of Rites | 53 |
| Perpetual Lamp | 57 |
| Hymn to Jesus | 58 |
| Devotion to the Agonizing Heart of Jesus | 59 |
| Litany of the Most Holy Name of Jesus | 62 |
| Month of June | 65 |
| Devotion to the Blessed Sacrament | 90 |
| Devotion to the Most Holy Trinity | 99 |
| Jesus Crucified | 102 |
| On Devotion to the Blessed Virgin | 104 |
| Devotion to St. Joseph | 113 |
| Devotion to St. Aloysius | 118 |
| Devotion to the Holy Angels | 120 |
| Devotion to the Souls in Purgatory | 122 |
| Prayers at Mass | 132 |
| Scapular of the Sacred Heart | 152 |
| Litany of the Saints | 173 |
| Prayers to the Most Holy Wounds | 185 |

# INTRODUCTION.

Though devotion to the Sacred Heart of Jesus was of great antiquity in the Church, yet it was reserved to Blessed Margaret Mary Alacoque, of the order of the Visitation, to make this devotion public. During the octave of Corpus Christi, in the year 1690, our blessed Lord appeared to his devoted servant, and disclosing to her his heart, said: "Behold this Heart, which, notwithstanding the burning love for man with which it is consumed and exhausted, meets with no other return from the generality of Christians than sacrilege, contempt, indifference, and ingratitude, even in the sacrament of my love. But what pierces my heart most deeply is, that I am subjected to those insults by persons specially consecrated to my service. Wherefore, I require of you to cause the first Friday after the octave of the blessed sacrament to be dedicated to honor my Heart, by receiving the holy communion, and making an act of atonement to repair the many indignities which have been offered to the holy sacrament while exposed on the altars; and in return, I promise that this Heart shall be dilated to pour out in abundance the influence of divine love on all who shall render to it this honor, or cause it to be rendered." But what will it avail us to have listened to these so just complaints of our Saviour, if we are not moved with compassion, and generously resolved to testify our sorrow for our past indifference by honoring his Sacred Heart, and by repairing, as far as lies in our power, the insults to which his ardent desire to dwell with the children of men daily exposes him in the august sacrament of his love. If gratitude to the God who suffered such torments for our salvation does not incline us to accept his gracious invitation, and to rank ourselves among the number of his adorers, at least let the recollection of the many spiritual advantages to be derived from devotion to the Sacred Heart induce us to pray fervently and humbly, that he, who has himself declared that it was a last effort of his love for man that induced him to discover to them the treasures of his Heart, may infuse into our souls the great gift of true piety to his most Sacred Heart. Let us respond to the call of this adorable Heart. It longs to rescue and shield us from the arch-enemy of our salvation. If the recollection of your unworthiness discourage you, call to mind the words of your Saviour, "Come to me, all you that labor and are heavily burdened, and I will refresh you." Remember that the Sacred Heart, which is compassion itself, is ever open to receive and shelter the repentant sinner. If you are bowed down by sin or sorrow, if temptations assail you, or the sight of your many infidelities and frequent relapses induce you to despair, fly with confidence to this furnace of love, for there, and there alone, will you find joy and consolation. "O sweetest Jesus," says St. Bernard, "what riches do you not enclose in your Heart! How easy for us to enrich ourselves, since we possess in the holy eucharist this infinite treasure!" If you are anxious to make atonement to the eternal Father for your many acts of ingratitude to him, offer him the merits of his divine Son. "Honor the adorable Heart of Jesus, by constant acts of fervent devotion." says Lanspergius, "offer all your petitions to God through that divine Heart, unite your intentions and actions to its merits; for it is the rich treasury of heaven. In your troubles and perplexities seek refuge in the Sacred Heart, and be convinced that though all the world should forget and forsake you, Jesus will ever be your faithful friend, and his Heart your secure asylum." In the eucharist Jesus bestows on us the most precious gift which even a God can give—his own Sacred Heart; and the only return he requires from us is, that we should give him our hearts in exchange. "Son give me thy heart." Determine, then, to respond to the affectionate solicitation of your Saviour. Never let a day pass without performing some pious exercise in honor of his Sacred Heart. Our Lord himself directed St. Mechtilde to let her first act when she awoke be to salute his Sacred Heart, and to offer him her own. Frequently during the day make fervent aspirations in honor of the Sacred Heart. Assist devoutly at the holy sacrifice of the Mass, and endeavor, as far as lies in your power, to make atonement to Jesus for the many outrages he has received in the sacrament of his love. As the first Friday of the month is in a special manner devoted to honor the Sacred Heart, be careful to consecrate that day to the love of our blessed Saviour. Cause your name to be enrolled in the "Confraternity of the Sacred Heart of Jesus," which has been enriched by the Holy See with considerable indulgences. The duties are few and easy, and do not bind under pain of sin, but merely under forfeitures of the indulgences. They are but two in number. First, daily to recite, in honor of the Sacred Heart, the *Our Father*, *Hail Mary*, and *Creed*, with the following aspiration:

"O Heart of Jesus, grant that I may love thee daily more and more."

Second—To pass one hour before the blessed sacrament on any one day of the year selected by the member on his joining the association; that hour to be spent in prayer, to repair the outrages offered to the Sacred Heart in the holy eucharist. Go to communion on the day of your entrance into the confraternity, in order to gain the plenary indulgence granted on that occasion. Every associate should have in his house a picture of the Sacred Heart. Our Blessed Lord, speaking on this subject to Margaret Mary, says: "I am much pleased with the devotion the faithful show for my Heart, and for this reason I desire the picture thereof may be drawn and exposed, that by this so amiable a representation the hearts of men may be softened into repentance. I promise that such as, in a more particular manner, honor this picture, shall partake more amply of those graces with which my Heart is replenished."

We find in the Hearts of Jesus and Mary, light, love, fortitude, resignation, zeal, patience, peace, and rest.

### SALUTARY PRACTICES.

1. Carefully avoid all sin, for it is the only cause of sorrow to the Hearts of Jesus and Mary.
2. Perform all your devotions and actions in union with the Hearts of Jesus and Mary.
3. Beg all graces through their intercession, repeating frequently, and especially in time of temptation, the prayer, "Sweet Hearts of Jesus and Mary, be my refuge."

# PROMISES

**MADE BY OUR LORD JESUS CHRIST TO BLESSED MARGARET MARY ALACOQUE, IN FAVOR OF PERSONS DEVOTED TO HIS DIVINE HEART.**

1. "I will give them all the grace necessary for their state of life."
2. "I will establish peace in their families."
3. "I will console them in all their pains and trials."
4. "I will be their assured refuge in life and especially in death."
5. "I will shed abundant blessings upon all their undertakings."
6. "Sinners shall find in My Heart an infinite ocean of Mercy."
7. "Lukewarm souls will be rendered fervent."
8. "Fervent souls shall rise rapidly to greater perfection."
9. "I will bless every house in which an image of My Sacred Heart shall be exposed and honored."
10. "I will give to Priests the talent of moving the hardest hearts."
11. "The names of those who propagate this devotion shall be written in My Heart, from which they shall never be effaced."
12. "Publish, and cause it to be published, over all the world, that I will set no limits to My graces for those souls that come to seek them in this, My Heart."

## Act of Consecration to Sacred Heart of Jesus.

O Sacred Heart of Jesus, to thee I devote and offer up my life, thoughts, words, actions, pains and sufferings. My entire being shall henceforward only be employed in loving, serving, honoring and glorifying thee. Be thou, O most Sacred Heart, the sole object of my love, the protector of my life, the pledge of my salvation, and my secure refuge at the hour of death. Be thou, also, O most bountiful Heart, my justification at the throne of God, and screen me from his anger, which I have so justly merited. In thee I place all my confidence, and, convinced as I am of my own weakness, I rely entirely on thy compassionate mercy. Annihilate in me all that is displeasing and offensive to thy pure eyes. Imprint thyself like a divine seal on my heart, that I may ever remember my obligations, and never be separated from thee. May my name, also, I beseech thee, by thy tender goodness, ever be fixed and engraved in thee, O book of life; and may I be a victim consecrated to thy glory, ever burning with the flames of thy pure love, both in time and in eternity. In this I place all my happiness; this is all my desire, to live and die in no other quality, but that of thy devoted servant. Amen.

### Act of Consecration to the Sacred Heart of Jesus.

My loving Jesus, I (N. N.) give thee my heart, and I consecrate myself wholly to thee, out of the grateful love I bear thee, and as a reparation for all my unfaithfulness to grace; and I purpose, with thine aid, never to sin again.

Plenary Indulgence once a month, if said daily; 100 days of Indulgence once a day.

### The Little Chaplet.

Deus in adjutorium, etc.

Incline unto mine aid, etc.

I. **Most** loving Jesus! my heart leaps for joy in thinking on thy loving sacred heart, all tenderness and sweetness for sinful man; and with trust unbounded, it never doubts thy ready welcome. Ah, me! my sins! how many and how great! With Peter and Magdalen, in tears, I bewail and abhor them, because they are an offence to thee, my sole and chief good. Grant me, oh, grant me pardon for them all! O may I die, I beseech thee, by thy loving heart, may I die rather than offend thee, and may I live only to correspond to thy love!

Say the *Our Father* once, the *Glory be to the Father* five times: and then:

O sweetest heart of Jesus! I implore
That I may ever love thee more and more.

II. My Jesus! I bless thy most humble heart; and I give thanks to thee, who, in making it my model, not only dost urge me, with much pressing, to imitate it, but, at the cost of so many humiliations, dost thyself stoop to point me out the path, and smooth for me the way to follow thee. **Foolish** and ungrateful that I am, how have I wandered far away from thee! Mercy my Jesus, mercy! Away, hateful pride and love of worldly honor! With lowly heart I wish to follow thee, my Jesus, through humiliations and the cross, and thus to gain peace and salvation. Only be thou at hand to strengthen me, and I will ever bless thy Sacred Heart.

*Our Father* once, *Glory be to the Father* five times.

O sweetest Heart of Jesus, etc.

III. My Jesus! I marvel at thy most patient heart, and I thank thee for all those wondrous examples of unwearied patience which thou didst leave me to guide me on my way. It grieves me that I have still to reproach myself with my extravagant delicacy, shrinking from the slightest pain. O pour, then, into my heart, dear Jesus, eager and enduring love of suffering and of the cross, of mortification and of penance, that, following thee to Calvary, I may with thee attain to glory, and to the joys of paradise!

*Our Father* once, *Glory be to the Father* five times.

O sweetest Heart of Jesus, etc.

IV. Dear Jesus! at the sight of thy most gentle heart, I shudder to see how unlike mine is to thine, since at a shadow, at a look, at a word of opposition, I fret and grieve. O, then, pardon my excesses, and give me grace, that in every contradiction, I may follow the example of thy unchangeable meekness, and so enjoy an everlasting holy peace.

*Our Father* once, *Glory be to the Father* five times.

O sweetest Heart of Jesus, etc.

V. Sing praise to Jesus for his most generous heart, the conqueror of death and hell; yet never wilt thou reach its due with all thy praise. More than ever am I confounded, looking upon my coward heart, which, through human respect, dreads even a passing word. Courage, my soul! it shall be so with thee no more. My Jesus, I pray thee for such strength that, fighting and conquering on earth, I may one day rejoice triumphantly with thee in heaven.

*Our Father* once, *Glory be to the Father* five times.

O sweetest Heart of Jesus, etc.

Let us turn to Mary, consecrating ourselves to her more and more, and, trusting in her maternal heart, let us say to her:

By the precious gifts of thy sweetest heart, obtain for me, great Mother of my God, and my Mother Mary, a true and lasting devotion to the Sacred Heart of Jesus, thy well-beloved Son, that, united in every thought and affection with that heart, I may fulfil all the duties of my state of life with ready heart, serving my Jesus ever more, but especially on this day.

*V.* Cor Jesu flagrans amore nostri.

*R.* Inflamma cor nostrum amore tui.

### OREMUS.

Illo nos igne, quæsumus, Domine, Spiritus Sanctus inflammet, quem Dominus noster Jesus Christus e penetralibus cordis sui misit in terram et voluit vehementur accendi. Qui tecum vivit et regnat in unitate ejusdem, Spiritus Sancti Deus, per omnia sæcula sæculorum. Amen.

*V.* Heart of Jesus burning with love for us.

*R.* Inflame our hearts with love of thee.

### LET US PRAY.

Lord, we beseech thee, let thy Holy Spirit kindle in our hearts that fire of charity which our Lord Jesus Christ, thy Son, sent forth from his inmost heart upon this earth and willed that it should burn with vehemence. Who liveth and reigneth with thee, in the unity of the same Holy Spirit, God, forever and ever. Amen.

## The Litany of the Sacred Heart.

Lord, have mercy on us.
Christ, have mercy on us.
Lord, have mercy on us.
Christ, hear us.
Christ, graciously hear us.

God, the Father of Heaven, }
God the Son, Redeemer of the world,
God the Holy Ghost,
Holy Trinity, one God,
Heart of Jesus,
Heart of Jesus, hypostatically united to the Eternal Word,
Heart of Jesus, sanctuary of the divinity, and tabernacle of the most holy Trinity,
Heart of Jesus, temple of sanctity and fountain of all graces,
Heart of Jesus, most meek and humble,
Heart of Jesus, most chaste and obedient,
Heart of Jesus, furnace of love and source of all contrition, } *Have mercy on us.*

Heart of Jesus, treasure of wisdom and goodness,
Heart of Jesus, throne of mercy and abyss of all virtues,
Heart of Jesus, sorrowful in the garden, and spent with a bloody sweat,
Heart of Jesus, saturated with reproaches, and consumed for our sins,
Heart of Jesus, made obedient even unto the death of the cross,
Heart of Jesus, pierced with a lance, and the refuge of sinners,
Heart of Jesus, fortitude of the just, and comfort of the afflicted,
Heart of Jesus, strength of the tempted, and terror of the devils,
Heart of Jesus, sanctification of hearts, and perseverance of the good,
Heart of Jesus, hope of the dying, joy of the blessed, and delight of all the saints,

*Have mercy on us.*

Lamb of God, &c. (*three times.*)

*V.* O most Sacred Heart of Jesus, have mercy on us.

*R.* That we may worthily love Thee with our whole hearts.

*Let us Pray.*

O God! Who out of Thy immense love hast given to the faithful the most Sacred Heart of Thy Son, our Lord, as the object of Thy tender affection; grant, we beseech Thee, that we may so love and honor this pledge of Thy love on earth, as by it to merit the love of Thee and Thy gift and be eternally loved by Thee and this most blessed Heart in heaven; through the same Jesus Christ, our Lord. Amen.

---

Through Thy Sacred Heart, O Jesus! overflowing with all sweetness, we recommend to Thee ourselves and all our concerns, our friends, benefactors, parents, our relations, our superiors and our enemies; take under thy protection this house, city and country; extend Thy care to all such as lie under any affliction, and to those who labor in the agony and pangs of death; cast an eye of compassion on the obstinate sinner, and more particularly on the poor suffering souls in purgatory, as also on those who are engaged and united with us in the holy confederacy of honoring and worshipping Thee. Bless these in particular, O divine Jesus! and bless them according to the extent of Thy infinite goodness, mercy and charity. Amen.

### Ejaculation.

May the Heart of Jesus in the most Blessed Sacrament be praised, adored and loved with grateful affection, at every moment, in all the tabernacles of the world, even to the end of time.

Amen.

An indulgence of 100 days, once a day.—Pius IX., Feb. 29, 1868.

## DEVOTION TO THE GUARD OF HONOR.

Compassionate Christians, friends of the Divine Heart, come with your love and your Gratitude, to Console, in the ranks of the Guard of Honour, This Heart that receives alas! so much indifference.

# PIOUS ASSOCIATION

#### OF THE

# GUARD OF HONOR

#### OF THE

## SACRED HEART OF JESUS,

Erected canonically in the Church of the Religious of the Visitation, St. Marie de Bourg (Ain), in the Church of SS. Vincent and Anastasia, at Rome, etc. Enriched with indulgences by his Holiness Pius IX. Approved by a great number of Archbishops and Bishops.

PROTECTORS :—*Our Lady of the Sacred Heart ; S. Joseph; S. Francis de Sales; S. Francis of Assisi; B. Margaret Mary.*

My heart expecteth reproach and misery. And I looked for one that would grieve together with Me, but there was none; and for one that would comfort Me, and I found none. Ps. 68.

## Renewal of Enrolment

Divine Jesus, my Saviour and my King, I renew with all my heart the resolution that I have made to LOVE, TO GLORIFY, TO CONSOLE YOUR ADORABLE HEART in the ranks of its Guard of Honor.

Grant, good Master, to make me each day more loving, more devoted, and more faithful; I ask of You this same grace for all of my Associates, through the sweetest Heart of Your Immaculate Mother. Amen.

## General Indulgences

The Guard of Honor, enriched by his Holiness Pius IX. with all the indulgences granted to the Archconfraternity of the Sacred Heart established in Rome, has, moreover, been gratified by an Apostolic Brief, dated April 7th, 1865, which grants to the Associates the following Indulgences:

1. An Indulgence of seven years and seven quarantines for the Hour of Guard each day.

2. An Indulgence of one hundred days for each of the other hours that the Associates may consecrate in the same way to the Heart of Jesus.

3. Plenary Indulgence once a month (the day may be chosen, ordinary conditions), when one has been faithful in making his Hour of Guard during the month. (Applicable to the souls in Purgatory.)

## SACRED HEART.

To belong to the Guard of Honor and to gain the Indulgences attached to it, it is necessary—

1. To be enrolled by the Head of the Work or by one of the Directors or Zelators.
2. To be recorded on a Clock of the Sacred Heart.
3. To make one's Hour of Guard.
4. To commence one's Hour as soon as one discovers that he has forgotten it.

It is DURING HIS HOUR OF GUARD that each Associate is urged to offer the chalice of benediction to the Most Adorable Trinity. He ought, then, during that hour, to renew without ceasing the Most Precious Offering of the Blood and Water flowing from the Wound of the Heart of Jesus; and this may be done mentally without being noticed, in going, in coming, in working, in suffering, in conversing; even, in fact, by each beating of the heart.

### The Most Precious Offering.

Heavenly Father! accept as a propitiation for the needs of the Church, and in reparation for the sins of men, the most precious drops of Blood and Water flowing from the divine Wound of the Heart of Jesus, and grant us mercy.—*Forty days' Indulgence.*

Our Lady of the S. Heart, protect the Guard of Honor.

### Object of the Association.

It is to respond to the sorrowful complaint of our Lord that the Guard of Honor has been organized.

The members who compose it shall, by their *devotedness* and their *love*, strive to console the Heart of Jesus, drowned in grief at the forgetfulness and ingratitude of men, for whom he suffered so much! whom he loves so ardently! and by whom he is so little loved!

Like respectful and loving children who try to console their tender Father, and to make amends to him for all that their ungrateful and unnatural brothers make him suffer, the Guards of Honor succeed each other by turns before their Saviour Jesus, to offer to his most tender Heart, respect, love, devotedness and consolation.

### Organization of the Association.

The Associates choose, once for all, a convenient hour of the day for this devotion. At the beginning of this hour of guard, without in any way changing their ordinary occupations, the Associates station themselves in spirit at the *Post of love*—the Tabernacle; there they offer to Jesus all their thoughts, words, actions, sufferings, and, above all, the desire they have to console his tender Heart, by their fidelity and their love. During the course of the hour, the Associates try to think a little oftener of our Lord, make at least an act of love, and, if they can, a little sacrifice. But nothing, absolutely nothing, is prescribed or of obligation; nothing but a good will is required, the Associates being free to follow the impulse of their hearts and their piety in sanctifying this blessed hour.

NOTE.—If the Associates forget their hour of guard, they can resume it as soon as they perceive the omission.

*The Heart of Jesus will heap grace upon grace, blessing upon blessing, on those faithful and compassionate souls who will fulfil this mission of devotedness and love.*

### Offering of the Hour of Guard.

Divine Jesus, my most sweet Saviour, I offer thee this hour of guard; during which, in union with (*here name the patrons of the hour chosen*) I desire most particularly to love thee, to glorify thee, and, above all, to console thy Adorable Heart for the forgetfulness and ingratitude of men. Accept, to this end, my thoughts, words, actions, and sufferings. Above all, receive my heart, which I give thee, without reserve, entreating thee to consume it in the fire of thy pure love.

May the Sacred Heart of Jesus be everywhere loved.

(*One hundred days' Indulgence for this aspiration.*)

O my Jesus, I desire to love thee during this hour, for all those hearts which do not love thee.

All for the Heart of Jesus through the Heart of Mary.

Our Lady of the Sacred Heart, protect the Guard of Honor!

Your Patrons chosen for the hour } 1 2 3

# OFFICE OF THE SACRED HEART OF JESUS.

## *Matins.*

Our Father, etc.   Hail Mary, etc.

*V.* Open my lips, O Lord.

*R.* And my mouth shall declare thy praise.

*V.* O God come to my aid.

*R.* O Lord, make haste to help me.

Glory be to the Father, etc.

From all eternity the heart of Jesus hath loved us; come, let us adore it.

## *Hymn.*

Sweet Jesus, may thy sacred heart
  My hope and refuge be;
There may I learn the heavenly art
  Of living but for thee.

This fountain of thy sacred heart,
  The source of love most pure,
To those who dwell from sin apart
  Affords a refuge sure.

*Anthem.*

Come to me, all you who labor and are heavy burdened, and I will refresh you. Take up my yoke, and learn of me, for I am meek and humble of heart.

*V.* I will make an everlasting covenant with my people.

*R.* I will unceasingly load them with blessings.

*V.* Lord, hear my prayer.

*R.* And let my cry come unto thee.

*Prayer.*

Grant, O my Jesus, that in honoring thy sacred heart, we may learn to practise meekness and humility, obtain the peace thou hast promised, and find rest to our souls. We beg of thee this grace; who livest and reignest with the Father and the Holy Ghost, world without end. Amen.

*V.* Lord, hear my prayer

*R.* And let my cry ascend to thy divine heart.

*V.* Let us bless the Lord.

*R.* Thanks be to God.

May the souls of the faithful departed, through the mercy of God, rest in peace. Amen.

### *Lauds.*

*V.* O God, come, etc.   *R.* Lord, etc. Glory, etc., as above.

> Thy heart with heavenly love's pure glow
>   Cleanseth our sins away;
> Sweet Lord, thy gifts thou dost bestow
>   Upon us day by day.
>
> Alas! how cold we are to thee,
>   Though to thy heart so dear;
> From thy kind gifts how oft we flee,
>   Nor heed thy loving care!

### *Anthem.*

Our Lord, in the excess of his love and mercy, has redeemed us by the ignominious death of the cross.

*V.* Taste and see how sweet is the Lord.
*R.* Happy those who bear his yoke from their early infancy.
*V.* Lord, hear, etc.   **Prayer: Grant, O Jesus,** as at Matins.

*Prime.*

*V.* O God, come, etc. *R.* Lord, make haste, etc. Glory, etc., as above.

> Within that sacred heart's pure shrine
> To the Most High doth plead
> Ever for us the Word divine,
> In all our earthly need.
>
> And day by day the Lamb is slain;
> The Lord of heaven above
> On lowly altars doth remain,
> The victim of his love.

*Anthem.*

My delight is to be with the children of men. Happy those who keep my commandments.

*V.* How good and merciful is the heart of Jesus!

*R.* How sweet it is to us to love and celebrate his mercies.

*V.* Lord, hear, etc. Prayer: Grant, O Jesus, etc.

*Terce.*

*V.* O God, come, etc. *R.* Lord, make haste, etc. Glory, etc.

The lance that pierced our Saviour's side
  Reveal'd a source of grace;
O then rejoice! for that pure tide
  Can all thy sins efface.

God calls us to his mercy's fount;
  Sweetly our love he claims,
Nor speaks, as once on Sinai's mount,
  In thunder and in flames.

*V.* Jesus having loved his own.
*R.* He loved them unto the end.
*V.* Lord, hear, etc.   Prayer: **Grant,** O Jesus, as at Matins.

*Sext.*

*V.* O God, come, etc.   *R.* Lord, make haste, etc.   Glory, etc.

O heart, of every grace the source,
  Of all God's gifts the best;
Unto the sinner strength and force,
  Refreshment, hope, and rest.

Sinner, arise! Ah! how canst thou
  So cold and tepid be?
Justice gives place to mercy now,
  When Jesus pleads for thee.

*Anthem.*

I have planted thee for my most beautiful vineyard, and thou hast proved very bitter to me.

*V.* I have watched over my chosen ones; I have loaded them with blessings.

*R.* And they have despised me.

*V.* Lord, hear, etc.  Prayer: Grant, O Jesus, as at Matins.

*None.*

*V.* O God, come, etc.  *R.* Lord, make haste, etc.  Glory, etc.

> Wisdom divine doth ever dwell
>   Within thy sacred heart;
> The waters, then, of that pure well
>   Sweet Lord, to us impart.
>
> Great Fount of truth, our souls inspire,
>   Each erring thought reclaim;
> Sweet source of mercy, with thy fire
>   Do thou our hearts inflame.

*Anthem.*

Those who seek me shall find me. If any one love me, I will love him, and will manifest myself to him.

*V.* O my soul, bless the Lord.

*R.* And never forget the graces with which he has filled thee.

*V.* Lord, hear, etc. Prayer: Grant, O Jesus, as at Matins.

### *Vespers.*

*V.* O God, come, etc. *R.* Lord, make haste, etc. Glory, etc.

O sacred heart, sweet source from whence
   A stream of life e'er flows;
The weary soul may draw from thence
   Refreshment and repose.

Hére may we find a spot secure
   From sin and vain alarm;
Here may we taste for evermore
   Thy love's consoling balm.

### *Anthem.*

You shall draw waters with joy from the fountains of the Saviour. Sing hymns to the Lord, because he has shown forth his greatness. Proclaim his magnificence throughout the world.

*V.* You who are my disciples, will you also abandon me?

*R.* Lord, to whom shall we go? Thou hast the words of eternal life.

*V.* Lord, hear, etc., with the prayer: Grant, O Jesus.

### *Complin.*

*V.* Convert us, O God, our Saviour.
*R.* And turn away thy anger from us.

> O heart of Jesus, may we feel
>   Thy pure consuming fire:
> Kindle in us thy ardent zeal,
>   Be thou our soul's desire.

> Absorb, dear Lord, our hearts in thine,
>   Let us with thee remain;
> Nor ever may our souls incline
>   To earth's vain joys again.

### *Anthem.*

I live, now not I, but Christ liveth in me. He has loved me, and delivered himself to death for me.

*V.* Come to me, all you who love me.
*R.* And I will enrich you with my blessings.

*V.* Lord, hear, etc. Prayer: Grant, O Jesus, etc., as at Matins.

## Dwellings in the Sacred Heart of Jesus.

#### SUNDAY.

Enter through the immaculate heart of Mary, into the open Heart of Jesus, *as into a furnace of love,* in order to purify yourself therein. with all the faithful, from all the stains with which you have been sullied in the course of the past week, and destroy this life of sin, that you may live more and more a life of pure love. Let this day be devoted to paying a special tribute to the holy Trinity, in union with the whole Church, by a fervent assiduity at its devout exercises.

#### MONDAY.

Enter through the immaculate Heart of Mary, into the Sacred Heart of Jesus, in order to confine yourself therein with the truly faithful, *as in a prison of love,* and to share in the bitter sorrow in which this holy Heart was steeped, considering yourself as a criminal who desires to appease his judge by manifesting regret for his faults, and by making satisfaction to justice; you must be content to remain the whole day so strictly bound and tied, that you will only have liberty to love with, and, like Jesus, having no longer any light or movement but that of pure love, by which he himself is held captive and without movement in the adorable sacrament of the altar. By the merits of this divine captivity, you will beg for the deliverance of the souls in purgatory, and perform all your actions this day in a *spirit of penance.*

### TUESDAY.

Enter, through the immaculate heart of Mary, into the Sacred Heart of Jesus, *as into a school of which you are one of the faithful disciples.* This is the school in which the science of the saints and that of pure love is acquired and where all worldly science is forgotten. Listen attentively to the voice of your Master, who says to you : *Learn of me to be meek and humble of heart, and you will find rest for your soul.* You must this day exercise yourself in the practice of humility.

### WEDNESDAY.

Enter, by means of the immaculate heart of Mary, into the Sacred Heart of Jesus, *as a traveler into a ship*: his pure love is the pilot appointed to conduct you happily over the stormy sea, through which you must pass in order to arrive at the port. The tempests and rocks which you have to fear, are the rebellious motions of self-will, and an inordinate attachment to the flesh and to creatures. From these dangers the divine Pilot will preserve you, provided that you intrust the conduct of everything to him. Endeavor during this day to excite yourself to confidence in God.

### THURSDAY.

Enter, through the immaculate heart

of Mary, into the Sacred Heart of Jesus, *as a friend invited to the feast of his friend.* You will find there delights ready prepared for you, far surpassing your desires and your expectations: the friend who receives you is as liberal as he is tender: he will say to you, *All that is mine is also thine:* my dolors, my merits, my riches, my glory. Love makes these goods common between us; but liberality should be reciprocal; and I desire also to possess thee entirely, without reserve, without division. Be not ungrateful, and remember to perform all your actions this day in a spirit of gratitude and love.

### FRIDAY.

Enter into the immaculate heart of Mary, in order to meditate therein on the love of Jesus nailed to the cross, and bringing you forth in grace with infinite suffering. Then go and repose on the Heart of your Saviour as a child on the bosom of its mother, seeking there, and there only, for consolation and perfect security, with that sweet confidence of a child, who well knows that its mother will never abandon it. Endeavor to pass this day in a spirit of indifference to all the events of this life, in union with Jesus; obedient to his Father, even unto death, and to the death of the cross.

### SATURDAY.

Enter, through the immaculate heart of Mary, into the Sacred Heart of Jesus, *as a victim just arrived at the temple where it is about to be immolated*, and which is presented to the sacrificator: this divine Priest, by spiritually killing it, will destroy in it the animal life; and then, by consuming it in the fire of love, he will restore it to a new life wholly divine. Rejoice while performing the duty of the holocaust; love to die to the world and to earthly things; love to be consumed for the glory of the Almighty, by the desire of that life of love which consists only in sacrifice. Thrice happy would you be, if you might soon be able to say with truth: "No, it is not I who live, I am dead; but it is Jesus Christ who lives in me by his love." It is in him and *by him that I act, that I suffer, and that I love.* Endeavor during this day to practise abnegation of self-will, saying with St. Paul: *Quotidie morior.*

### Prayer.

O Jesus, living in Mary! come and live in thy servants, in the spirit of thy holiness, in the fulness of thy might, in the truth of thy virtues, in the perfection of thy ways, in the communion of thy mysteries; subdue every hostile power in thy spirit for the glory of the Father. Amen.

His Holiness, Pope Pius IX., Oct. 14, 1859, granted to all who, with at least contrite heart and devotion, shall say this prayer, 300 DAYS' INDULGENCE, once a day.

## Ejaculations.

**My sweetest Jesus, be not my Judge, but my Saviour.**

> 50 days' indulgence, once a day.
> Plenary indulgence, once a year.

**My Jesus, mercy.**

> 100 days' indulgence, each time.

**Jesus Christ be praised.**

> 100 days' indulgence.

### Prayer to the Sacred Heart of Jesus.

Most holy Heart of Jesus, hear me!
Let the fire of thy heart animate me!
Let the thorny crown of thy heart render me patient!
Let the wounds of thy heart pierce me!
Let the blood of thy heart make atonement for me!
Let the light of thy heart enlighten me!
Let the homage of thy heart sanctify me!
Let the mercy of thy heart encircle me!
Let the love of thy heart bless me!
My heart I unite to thine in love!
O Heart of Jesus! invite me to thee, that with all the angels and saints,
I may praise thee, here for a time, but there for eternity.

## JESUS.

I need thee, precious Jesus,
    I need a friend like Thee;
A friend to soothe and sympathize,
    A friend to care for me.

I need Thy Heart, sweet Jesus,
    To feel each anxious care;
I long to tell my every want,
    And all my sorrows share.

I need Thy Blood, sweet Jesus,
    To wash each sinful stain;
To cleanse this sinful soul of mine,
    And make it pure again.

I need Thy Wounds, sweet Jesus,
    To fly from perils near,
To shelter in these hallowed clefts
    From every doubt and fear.

I need Thee, sweetest Jesus,
    In Thy Sacrament of Love,
To nourish this poor soul of mine
    With the treasures of Thy love.

I'll need Thee, sweetest Jesus,
    When death's dread hour draws nigh,
To hide me in Thy Sacred Heart,
    Till wafted safe on high.

*Ejaculation.*

O sweetest Heart of Jesus I implore that I may ever love Thee more and more.

(100 *days' indulgence.*)

### Visit to a Picture of the Sacred Heart.

Pius VI., to increase devotion to the Sacred Heart of Jesus, granted an *Indulgence of seven years and seven quarantines* as often as, with contrite hearts and devotion, they visit a picture of the Sacred Heart of Jesus, exposed for public veneration in a church or oratory, or altar, and pray there for some time for the intention of his Holiness.

### Feast of the Sacred Heart.

The Sovereign Pontiff, Pius VII., by a rescript from the Office of the Secretary of Memorials, July 7, 1815, granted:

A Plenary Indulgence to all the faithful who, being truly penitent, after confession and communion, shall visit any church or public oratory in which the feast of the Sacred Heart is celebrated, and pray there for the intention of the Sovereign Pontiff.

He granted also permission to transfer the feast, with leave of the ordinaries of the respective places, to any other day in the year.

---

### The Month of the Sacred Heart.

His Holiness, Pope Pius IX., by a decree of the S. Congr. of Indulgences, May 8, 1873, granted to all the faithful who, during the month of June, either in public or in private, shall, with at least contrite heart, say some special prayers, or perform some pious acts in honor of the most Sacred Heart of Jesus:

An Indulgence of seven years, once a day.

A Plenary Indulgence, on any one day of the month, provided that, being truly penitent, after confession and communion, they shall visit some church or public oratory, and pray there devoutly, for some time, for the intention of his Holiness.

An Indulgence of One Hundred Days, once a day.

## Novena in Honor of the Sacred Heart of Jesus.

The Sovereign Pontiff, Pius VII., by a rescript of the S. Congr. of Indulgences, Jan. 13, 1818, granted to all the faithful who, at any time during the year, shall, with at least contrite heart and devotion, make the novena in honor of the Sacred Heart of Jesus, composed by Father Borgo of the Society of Jesus, or any other they may prefer:

An Indulgence of Three Hundred Days, every day.

A Plenary Indulgence on the day immediately after the novena, or during the octave, provided that, being truly penitent, after confession and communion, they shall visit a church, or public oratory, and pray there for the intention of the Sovereign Pontiff.

## Novena to the Sacred Heart of Jesus.

In union with Our Lady of the Sacred Heart, and St. Joseph, Patron of the Universal Church.

To be made before the First Friday of each month.

### GENERAL INTENTIONS.

*To make reparation for—*

    1st. Impiety and Indifference.
    2nd. Blasphemies.
    3rd. Profanation of the Sacraments.
    4th. The abuse of graces.

*To pray for—*

    1st. Propagation of Devotion to the Sacred Heart of Jesus.
    2nd. An intimate knowledge of our Lord Jesus Christ.
    3rd. The Pope and the Church.
    4th. An increase of Faith, Hope and Charity.
    5th. The grace of a Happy Death.

**SPECIAL INTENTIONS—EACH ONE CAN SPECIFY.**

N. B.—This Novena should be commenced so as to conclude on Thursday evening previous to the first Friday of the Month. If a Sacramental Communion be impossible, a Spiritual Communion should be made, and an act of Reparation and Consecration to the Sacred Heart of Jesus.

*Prayers of the Novena—Union with the Sacred Heart of Jesus.*

Profound Adoration of the Heart of Jesus,
Ardent Love of the Heart of Jesus,
Fervent Zeal of the Heart of Jesus,
Reparation of the Heart of Jesus,
Thanksgiving of the Heart of Jesus,
Confidence of the Heart of Jesus,
Inflamed Prayers of the Heart of Jesus,
Eloquent Silence of the Heart of Jesus,
Humility of the Heart of Jesus,
Obedience of the Heart of Jesus,
Meekness and Grace of the Heart of Jesus,

} *unite with you.*

Ineffable Goodness of the Heart of Jesus,
Universal Charity of the Heart of Jesus,
Profound Recollection of the Heart of Jesus,
Tender Solicitude of the Heart of Jesus for the Conversion of Sinners,
Intimate Union of the Heart of Jesus with his heavenly Father,
Intentions, Desires and Will of the Heart of Jesus,

} *I unite with you.*

*Invocations to the Sacred Heart of Jesus.*

Love of the Heart of Jesus, inflame my heart.
Charity of the Heart of Jesus, flow into my heart.
Strength of the Heart of Jesus, support my heart.
Mercy of the Heart of Jesus, pardon my heart.
Patience of the Heart of Jesus, grow **not weary of my heart.**

Kingdom of the Heart of Jesus, be in my heart.
Wisdom of the Heart of Jesus, teach my heart.
Will of the Heart of Jesus, dispose of my Heart.
Zeal of the Heart of Jesus, consume my heart.
Immaculate Virgin, pray for us to the Sacred Heart of Jesus.
Adorable Trinity, we thank you for all the favors you have conferred on your servant, Blessed Margaret Mary, and through her intercession we hope to obtain the graces we ask for in this Novena.

### Prayer of Blessed Margaret Mary.

Eternal Father, permit me to offer to you the Heart of your well-beloved Son, Jesus Christ, as he offers himself to you in sacrifice. Receive this oblation for me, together with all the desires, sentiments, affections, movements and acts of this Sacred Heart. They are all mine, since he immolates himself for me, and henceforth I wish to have no desires but his. Receive them in satisfaction for my sins, and in thanksgiving for all your benefits. Receive them, that through his merits, you may grant me all the graces necessary for me, especially the grace of Final Perseverance. Receive them as so many acts of love, adoration and praise, which I offer to your Divine Majesty, since it is by the Heart of Jesus you are worthily honored and glorified. Amen.

### A Devout Aspiration to the Sacred Heart.

Most amiable Heart of Jesus! beloved object of our most tender affections! may all honor, glory, love and benediction be ever given to Thee. Be Thou our comfort in adversity, our guide in prosperity, our safety in dangers, and protection against all our enemies, visible and invisible. Amen.

## Rosary of the Sacred Heart.

This Rosary is said in honor of the five wounds, and the ordinary beads are used.

*A.—Instead of Apostles' Creed, say:*

Soul of Christ, sanctify me:
Body of Christ, save me:
Blood of Christ, inebriate me:
Water from the side of Christ, wash me:
Passion of Christ, strengthen me:
O good Jesus, hear me:
Within thy wounds hide me:
Permit me not to be separated from thee.
From the malignant enemy defend me:
In the hour of my death call me,
And bid me come to thee,
That, with thy saints, I may praise thee:
For ever and ever. Amen.

300 days' indulgence—seven years and seven quarantines, when said after holy communion.

*B.—Instead of the Our Father, say:*

"Jesus, meek and humble of Heart, make my heart like unto Thine."—(300 days' indulgence.)

## SACRED HEART.

*C.—Instead of the Hail Mary, say:*

"Sweet Heart of Jesus, be my love."—(300 *days' indulgence.*)

*D.—Instead of the Glory be to the Father, say:*

"Sweet Heart of Mary, be my salvation."—(300 *days' indulgence.*)

*E.—To conclude, say:*

"Most holy Heart of Jesus, have mercy on us."—(100 *days' indulgence.*)

"Immaculate Heart of Mary, pray for us."—(100 *days' indulgence.*)

"May the Sacred Heart of Jesus be loved everywhere."—(100 *days' indulgence.*)

---

### ACT OF CONSECRATION TO THE SACRED HEART OF JESUS.

**Approved by Decree of the Sacred Congregation of Rites, April 22d, 1875.**

O Jesus! my Redeemer and my God! notwithstanding the great love Thou hast for men, for whose redemption Thou didst pour out all Thy precious blood,

Thou art so little loved by them; Thou art even grievously offended and outraged by them, especially by blasphemy and the profanation of holy feasts! Ah! would that I could make to Thy Divine Heart some satisfaction; that I could repair the great ingratitude and neglect with which Thou art treated by the greater part of mankind! O, that I could obtain from It the conversion of sinners, and arouse from their indifference so many others, who, though they have the happiness to belong to Thy Church, have not at heart the interests of Thy glory and of the Church, Thy Spouse! O, that I could obtain from It that those Catholics also, who still show themselves such by many external acts of charity, but, obstinately clinging to their own opinions, refuse submission to the decisions of the Holy See, or cherish sentiments at variance with its teaching —would look to themselves, and come to the conviction that he who **refuses to hear the Church in everything, refuses to hear God who is with her.**

In order to attain these holy results, and also to obtain triumph and lasting peace for Thy Immaculate Spouse, the happiness and prosperity of Thy Vicar on earth; in order to obtain the fulfilment of his holy intentions, and also that the members of the clergy may sanctify themselves more and more, and may be pleasing in Thy sight; and for so many other intentions, which Thou, O my Jesus, knowest to be conformable to Thy divine will, and which may help in some way to the conversion of sinners and to the sanctification of the just, in order that we may all, one day, secure the eternal salvation of our souls; in fine, because I know, my Jesus, that I shall thus be doing a thing very pleasing to Thy most tender Heart—prostrate at Thy feet, in the presence of the most holy Virgin Mary and of the whole court of heaven, I solemnly acknowledge that, by every title of justice and gratitude, I belong wholly and only to Thee, my Redeemer, Jesus Christ, who art the only source of all good both in my body and my soul; and in union with the intention of the Sovereign Pontiff, I consecrate to Thy most Sacred Heart myself and all that I have. I wish to love and serve It alone with all my soul, with all my heart, with all my strength, making Thy will mine, and uniting all my sorrows to thine.

Lastly, as a public token of this consecration which I make, I declare solemnly to Thee, O my God, that in future, to the honor of the same Sacred Heart, I will observe, according to the laws of the Church, all the feasts of obligation, and procure their observance by all those over whom I may have any influence or authority.

And thus placing together, in Thy amiable Heart, all these holy desires and resolutions with which Thy grace inspires me, I trust that I may make some atonement to It for the many insults It receives from the ungrateful children of men, and may find happiness for my own soul and for the souls of all my brethren, in this life and in the next. **Amen.**

## The Perpetual Lamp.

**Note.** In many churches and chapels, by means of small contributions, a lamp is kept burning day and night before the picture of the Sacred Heart. The object and beautiful significance of this custom is the subject of the following hymn.

This Lamp, though plain and poor it be,
    Yet burneth day and night,
O Sacred Heart! to honor Thee,
    And sheds its mellow light.

And my poor heart, though far away,
    With ceaseless yearning turns,
To Thy dear shrine, with gentle ray,
    Where this lamp ever burns.

O Lord! in spirit prostrate there,
    I offer Thee its rays,
As adoration's constant prayer,
    Thanksgiving, love and praise.

And while through day with painful tramp,
    I plod my weary way,
Before Thy heart this little Lamp,
    For me shall homage pay.

When after toil repose I take,
    And night brings gentle sleep,
A loving vigil for my sake
    It evermore shall keep.

O, heart of Jesus! meek and mild,
    Accept this gift, though poor,
And grant the grace to me, Thy child,
    To love Thee more and more.

DEVOTION TO THE

## Hymn.

To you who live in grief and pain,
    Oppressed by guilt's dismay,
May heavenly peace return again,
    To chase your griefs away.

Jesus on high, to sinners kind,
    A victim doth appear;
O hasten His fond heart to find,
    And rest securely there.

Yes, 'tis His voice that sounds so sweet:
    Why, sinners, fly from Me?
Come, seek forgiveness at My feet,
    Your sins shall pardon'd be.

What heart did ever friendship prove
    Like His, so good and great?
Behold how His expiring love
    His Father doth entreat.

For you and me, nay, e'en for those
    Who bid His veins to bleed:
"Father, forgive my cruel foes."
    O, this was love indeed.

Jesus, that Heart, which with delight
    Fills the angelic train,
Doth sweetly thus our souls invite
    Thy mercy to obtain.

O, dry our tears, our bruises heal,
    To us Thy blood apply:
A new-formed heart in us reveal,
    Who for Thy bounty cry.

### DEVOTION TO THE

## AGONIZING HEART OF JESUS.

The end of this devotion is, *Firstly*, to honor the Sacred Heart of Jesus, enduring throughout his whole life, but above all, during His Passion, great interior sufferings for the salvation of souls.

*Secondly*, to obtain, by the merits of this long agony, a happy death for the 80,000 persons who expire each day in all parts of the world. This number is not exaggerated: it has been proven by experience.

### DAILY PRAYER,

#### FOR THE AGONIZING OF THE DAY;

*That is to say, for all those who may expire during the twenty-four hours.*

Most merciful Jesus, lover of souls! I pray thee, by the agony of thy Sacred Heart, and the dolors of thy immaculate mother, wash in thy blood the sinners of the whole world, who are now in their agony and are to die this day. Amen.

Heart of Jesus, once in agony, **pity the dying.**

Pius IX. granted 100 days' indulgence, each time, to those who recite the above prayer, and a plenary indulgence, once a month, on the ordinary conditions, to those who shall recite it at least three times a day, for a month together, at different hours of the day. (Feb. 2d, 1850.)

### PRACTICE.

Together with this prayer, offer up some of your daily actions to the agonizing Heart of Jesus, in behalf of those who are to die this day.

PRAY FOR THE DYING. To-day 80,000 persons must fall, cut down by the stroke of death!.... must appear at the dread tribunal of God!.... must begin an eternity of happiness or suffering!.... Alas! among this immense number how many thousands are perhaps in a state of mortal sin!

PRAY, COMPASSIONATE CHRISTIANS. The Heart of Jesus implores it of you, this Heart which has so loved you, this Heart which has suffered so much for you and for these poor souls. Pray! above all, for those sinners who are at the point of death. They need, to avoid hell, but one well-made confession, or one good act of contrition. Beg the Agonizing Heart of Jesus to grant them one or other of these graces. Beg it of Him without delay. Time flies! to-morrow it will be too late.

**Pray for the Dying.** They are your brethren in Jesus Christ, your relations, perhaps, your friends or your benefactors!

**Pray for the Dying**; and you will imitate our Lord Jesus Christ: you will save souls. What a holy mission!

**Pray for the Dying.** St. James says: Whoever aids his brother to correct the errors of his way shall save his soul from death and shall cover a multitude of sins.

**Pray for the Dying.** Some day they will pray for you when in your agony. What a consolation in those last terrible moments!

---

Spread this devotion to the Agonizing Heart of Jesus, introduce it into your families, into religious communities, and this Sacred Heart will bless you. If by the fervor of your prayers you succeed in saving one soul daily, at the end of a year this number would amount to 365 souls; at the end of ten years to 3,650 souls. What a harvest! What a crown for eternity!!

## Litany of the Most Holy Name of Jesus.

Lord, have mercy on us,
Christ, have mercy on us.
Lord, have mercy on us.
Jesus, hear us.
Jesus, graciously hear us.
God, the Father of heaven.
God the Son, Redeemer of the world,
God the Holy Ghost,
Holy Trinity, one God,
Jesus, Son of the living God,
Jesus, splendor of the Father,
Jesus, brightness of eternal light,
Jesus, King of Glory,
Jesus, sun of justice,
Jesus, Son of the Virgin Mary,
Jesus, most amiable,
Jesus, most admirable,
Jesus, the mighty God,
Jesus, Father of the world to come,
Jesus, angel of the great council,
Jesus, most powerful,
Jesus, most patient,
Jesus, most obedient,
Jesus, meek and humble of heart,

} *Have mercy on us.*

Jesus, lover of chastity,
Jesus, lover of mankind,
Jesus, God of peace,
Jesus, author of life,
Jesus, model of virtues,
Jesus, zealous for souls,
Jesus, our God,
Jesus, our refuge,
Jesus, father of the poor,
Jesus, treasure of the faithful,
Jesus, good shepherd,
Jesus, true light,
Jesus, eternal wisdom,
Jesus, infinite goodness,
Jesus our way and our life,
Jesus, joy of the angels,
Jesus, King of the patriarchs,
Jesus, Master of the apostles,
Jesus, Teacher of the evangelists,
Jesus, strength of martyrs,
Jesus, light of confessors,
Jesus, purity of virgins,
Jesus, crown of all saints,

} *Have mercy on us.*

Be merciful, *spare us O Jesus.*
Be merciful, *graciously hear us, O Jesus.*

From all evil,
From all sin,
From all wrath,
From the snares of the devil,
From the spirit of fornication,
From everlasting death,
From neglect of thy inspirations,
Through the mystery of thy holy incarnation,
Through thy nativity,
Through thy infancy,
Through thy most divine life,
Through thy labors,
Through thy agony and passion,
Through thy cross and dereliction,
Through thy weariness and faintness,
Through thy death and burial,
Through thy resurrection,
Through thy ascension,
Through thy joys,
Through thy glory,

*Jesus, deliver us.*

Lamb of God, who takest away the sins of the world,
*Spare us, O Jesus.*
Lamb of God, who takest away the sins

of the world,
*Graciously hear us, O Jesus.*
Lamb of God, who takest away the sins of the world,
*Have mercy on us, O Jesus.*
Jesus, hear us.
Jesus, graciously hear us.

*Let us pray.*

O Lord Jesus Christ, who hast said, "Ask, and ye shall receive; seek, and ye shall find; knock, and it shall be open unto you; grant we beseech thee, to us who ask the gift of thy divine love, that we may love thee with our whole heart, in word and work, and never cease from showing forth thy praise.

Grant, O Lord, that we may have a perpetual fear and love of thy holy name; for thou never failest to direct and govern those whom thou hast instructed in thy true and solid love. Through our Lord, etc.

OFFERING OF THE MONTH.

O Sacred Heart of Jesus, source of every grace, virtue, and benediction, moved by that tender mercy of thine, which has so loved me even when I loved thee not; I hope that now, when I really do desire to love and serve thee, thou wilt still love and bless me. Accept, thou, O most injured and divine Heart, my desire of consecrating this month to thy special honor and imitation, and in reparation for the insults and neglects thou receivedst in the greatest pledge of thy Heart's love, the Holy Sacrament of our Altars. I offer thee my body, my health, labors, my life, my soul, and heart, and all that I have or am, to be employed purely for thy love. In giving thee my heart, through the Heart of thy Sacred Mother, I give thee but little, but it is all I have, and all that thou desirest. Take, then, my heart, change it, convert it, and purify it, and make it entirely thine. Amen.

### June 1st.

#### THE SACRED HEART OF JESUS THE CENTRE OF ALL HEARTS.

*Protectors for this day,*—The Holy Angels, and St. Joachim and St. Anne.

*General Protectors for the month,—* Mary and Joseph, the first and truest adorers of the Sacred Heart of Jesus.

### Practice.

Begin this month well. Offer yourself with Jesus and to Jesus, at the Offertory of the Holy Mass. Make the Act of Consecration to the Sacred Heart.

### Aspiration.

Sacred Heart of Jesus, I give myself wholly to thee.

### JUNE 2ND.

**THE SACRED HEART OF JESUS OUR VICTIM.**

*Protectors,—*The Archangels, and St. John, the Disciple of love.

### Practice.

At the Holy Sacrifice, this day, offer yourself as a victim, in union with the Sacred Heart of Jesus, and make the Act of Reparation to this Blessed Victim for your sins, especially ——— : do this with fervor and sincerity at the Offertory.

### Aspiration.

Sacred Heart of Jesus, Victim of my sins mercy! mercy!

### June 3rd.

#### THE SACRED HEART OF JESUS OUR RANSOM.

*Protectors.*—The Thrones, and St. Bonaventure.

### Practice.

Full reparation for any scandal or bad example you may have hitherto given. Try to ransom some poor soul from Purgatory, and labor and pray for the conversion of sinners. Have a Mass offered for these intentions, or assist at Mass as a true child of God.

### Aspiration.

"Shall I not live and die for him, who has lived and died for me." *St. F. de Sales.*

## June 4th.

**THE SACRED HEART OF JESUS PENITENT FOR OUR SINS.**

*Protectors,*—The Angel Gabriel, and Saints Peter, James, and John.

### Practice.

Make your confession in union with the penitent Heart of Jesus in Gethsemane. Beg of Jesus to give you a share of that sorrow which he felt in the Garden of Olives, for those sins of which you are going to accuse yourself.

### Aspiration.

"Not my will, but thine, be done." O! Sacred Heart of Jesus! pardon! mercy! conversion!

## June 5th.

**THE SACRED HEART OF JESUS OUR SACRIFICE.**

*Protectors,*—The Dominations, and St. Mary Magdalene.

### Practice.

Assist at Mass to day, in union with

the Holy Virgin Mother, the beloved Disciple, and the grateful penitent Magdalene, at the foot of the Cross, in the full spirit of sacrifice. Give up all that the Sacred Heart requires. Ask all that you wish with strong faith and unbounded confidence. Say the Litany of the Sacred Heart.

### Aspiration.

Heart of Jesus, made obedient even to the death of the Cross, have mercy on me.

### June 6th.

**The Sacred Heart of Jesus, the Author and Finisher of our Faith.**

*Protectors*,—The Powers, and St. Thomas, Apostle.

### Practice.

In the spirit of lively faith, say the Nicene or Apostles' Creed. Kiss often the Image of the Sacred Heart, begging lively faith, working by the charity of this loving Heart. Show forth your faith by your entire conduct.

### Aspiration.

Sacred Heart of Jesus, give me a lively and strong faith.

### June 7th.

**THE SACRED HEART OF JESUS OUR HOPE.**

*Protectors,*—The Principalities, and St. Augustine.

### Practice.

Perform all your actions this day, in the spirit of hope and confidence in the Sacred Heart of Jesus. Say the "Magnificat," to beg the virtue of hope.

### Aspiration.

Sacred Heart of Jesus, in thee will I hope.

### June 8th.

**THE SACRED HEART OF JESUS OUR LIGHT.**

*Protectors,*—The Virtues, and St. Teresa.

### Practice.

With all the fervour of your soul say

the Hymn of the Holy Spirit, earnestly begging light and strength to know and do God's will, according to your vocation. Resolve to be faithful to the particular Examen.

### Aspiration.

Lord, that I may see.

### JUNE 9TH.

**THE SACRED HEART OF JESUS OUR STRENGTH.**

*Protectors,*—The Cherubim, and St. Bernard.

### Practice.

Renounce, this day, before the image of the Sacred Heart of Jesus, all trust in yourself and in creatures. Say fervently, the Act of Consecration, to beg grace to begin, to do, and to suffer, all things in this great and powerful Heart.

### Aspiration.

Sacred, Omnipotent, Heart of Jesus, strengthen me in this hour.

## June 10th.

**THE SACRED HEART OF JESUS THE WAY, THE TRUTH AND THE LIFE.**

*Protectors*,—The Seraphim, and the Angels of the Association of St. Francis de Sales.

### Practice.

Earnestly beg this day, true devotion to the Sacred Heart of Jesus, "the Way, the Truth and the Life." Beg it every time the clock strikes, by a fervent elevation of the heart, and beg it through Mary and Joseph, the first lovers of this Divine Heart.

### Aspiration.

Sacred Heart of Jesus, our "Way, Truth, and Life," give me to know, love, and imitate thee.

## June 11th.

**THE SACRED HEART OF JESUS OUR KING.**

*Protectors*,—The Holy Guardian Angels, and St. Ignatius, and all the Saints of his Society.

### Practice.

Consecrate yourself with all the fervour of your soul, as did St. Ignatius to the Sacred Heart of Jesus, your glorious King and Captain. Often say with fervour the "Our Father," dwelling on the words "Thy Kingdom come."

### Aspiration.

Live, Jesus our King, and **Mary our Queen.**

## JUNE 12TH.

**THE SACRED HEART OF JESUS OUR MASTER.**

*Protectors,*—The Holy Angels of those who announce the word of God, and Sts. Xavier and Regis.

### Practice.

Say the Litany of St. Aloysius, and beg of him to obtain for you and your family true devotion to the Sacred Heart. On this day the Novena of St. Aloysius commences.

### Aspiration.

Master, I will follow thee whithersoever thou goest.

## June 13th.

**THE SACRED HEART OF JESUS OUR SCHOOL.**

*Protectors,*—The Holy Angels of our friends, and St. Thomas de Pazzi.

### Practice.

Take up in earnest the challenge of a Father of the Society of Jesus, "go," says he, "on trial to the School of the Sacred Heart of Jesus, for one fortnight, and if at the end of this time you perceive no improvement in your soul, I give you leave to go elsewhere." Say the Litany of the Sacred Heart, to beg meekness and humility.

### Aspiration.

Sacred Heart of Jesus, meek and humble, teach me thy own favorite lesson.

## June 14th.

**THE SACRED HEART OF JESUS, OUR BOOK.**

*Protectors,*—St. Michael, Archangel, and St. Gertrude.

### Practice.

For this day, spend a quarter of an hour reading the living book of the Sacred Heart of Jesus. If possible before the Blessed Sacrament, beg of Mary and Joseph to open for you. Perhaps the first words will be "Learn of me for I am Meek and Humble," or Child give me thy Heart." Make an act of faith before the Blessed Sacrament.

### Aspiration.

Mary, my true Mother, open to me and teach me to read, understand, and practice the book of life, the Sacred Heart of thy divine Son.

### JUNE 15TH.

#### THE SACRED HEART OF JESUS OUR DIRECTOR.

*Protectors,*—St. Raphael, and the Holy Disciples of the Sacred Heart, St. Francis Borgia, and St. John of God.

### Practice.

For this one day at least, (and perhaps you wish for the month), go to the Heart of Jesus, as to your Director, begging of him to let you know your faults and imperfections. Say the Litany of the Sacred Heart, to beg grace to do whatever Jesus may require of you.

### Aspiration.

Sacred Heart of Jesus, speak to my heart.

### JUNE 16TH.

**THE SACRED HEART OF JESUS OUR REFUGE.**

*Protectors,*—St. Stanislaus and St. Aloysius.

### Practice.

In all temptations and trials, flee for refuge into the Sacred Heart of Jesus; and though by your past infidelities you find it closed against you, "Fear not," go to Mary, and she will surely give you entrance. Say in the spirit of humble confidence, the "Our Father" and "Hail Mary."

### Aspiration.

Sacred Heart of Jesus, refuge of all the

miserable, protect me. Mary, refuge of sinners, pray for me your child.

### June 17th.

**THE SACRED HEART OF JESUS WOUNDED ON THE CROSS FOR OUR LOVE.**

*Protectors,*—The Angels of Sts. Aloysius and Stanislaus.

### Practice.

Honor by every means the wounded Hearts of Jesus and Mary. Make with fervour and compunction the act of Reparation to these blessed Hearts. Resolve with Catharine of Sienna, rather to die than ever again renew their sorrow by willful sin.

### Aspiration.

Precious blood flowing from the wounded Heart of Jesus, wash away my grievous sins, purify and invigorate me.

### June 18th.

**THE SACRED HEART OF JESUS OUR FRIEND.**

*Protectors,*—The Angels of the order of St. Domonic and Thomas of Aquin.

#### Practice.

In a visit to the Sacred Heart in the Holy Sacrament, examine well your heart; its attachments, aversons, desires, fears, and joys. Beg of Jesus to give you a new heart, a heart pure and detached from self and creatures. Honor, love, and serve all creatures for Jesus, and in Jesus.

#### Aspiration.

Sacred Heart of Jesus, true and only friend, receive me into thy friendship.

### June 19th.

#### THE SACRED HEART OF JESUS, THE ANGEL OF THE GREAT COUNCIL.

*Protectors,*—The Angel of our Diocese, and Sts. Charles and Liguori.

#### Practice.

In your daily affairs and occupations, beg the light of the Angel of the Great Council. Sometimes for a moment kneel before an image of the Sacred Heart, and say, "Lord, that I may see."

If you have the good custom of wearing a medal of the Sacred Heart, press it frequently to your heart and lips.

### Aspiration.

Sacred Heart of Jesus, Angel of the Great Council direct me.

### June 20th.

THE SACRED HEART OF JESUS OUR SOLITUDE.

*Protectors,*—The Angels of our Churches, and Sts. Benedict and Scholastica.

### Practice.

Spend this day in the spirit of reparation and gratitude to the Sacred Heart of Jesus, solitary on our altars. Visit it in this spirit, especially at the hour when you think it generally most solitary. Say the act of reparation to the Sacred Heart.

### Aspiration.

Sacred Heart of Jesus, silent and solitary, give me the spirit of interior life, all hidden in thee.

## June 21st.

#### THE SACRED HEART OF JESUS OUR ORATORY AND ALTAR.

*Protectors,*—The Angels of St. Aloysius and St. Stanislaus Kostka.

### Practice.

Say the Litany of the Sacred Heart, and beg the Spirit of prayer. "You wish for an altar on which to offer your sacrifices to God? Lay them on the Sacred Heart of Jesus," and beg of Mary and Joseph to present them in your name. Try to have as many sacrifices as you can. There can be no sanctity without mortification.

### Aspiration.

Blessed Heart of Jesus, be my Altar and my Oratory. Teach me how to pray.

## June 22nd.

#### THE SACRED HEART OF JESUS OUR TREASURE.

*Protectors,*—The Holy angels of our Family, and St. Ursula and Holy Companions.

### Practice.

Profit this day, at least, of the treassure in your hands, the Sacred Heart of Jesus. Enrich yourself, draw plentifully from this mine of grace, for yourself, and for all those who are near and dear to you; for poor sinners, for the souls in Purgatory, especially of the Holy Sacrifice. At the Offertory of the Holy Mass consecrate yourself anew to the Heart of Jesus, through Mary and Joseph. Make the act of Consecration.

### Aspiration.

Sacred Heart of Jesus, my Treasure, enrich my soul with thy graces.

## JUNE 23RD.

### THE SACRED HEART OF JESUS, OUR HOME AND DWELLING.

*Protectors,*—The Thrones, and St. John of the Cross.

### Practice.

Let the Heart of Jesus be your home and your dwelling. Try to prepare your

Heart for this great favor. Say the hymn of the Holy Spirit and the "Memorare," to beg light to know what bad habits and passions chiefly impede your entrance into the Heart of Jesus. Be faithful to the hours of entering in spirit this sacred dwelling; nine in the morning and four in the evening.

### Aspiration.

Who shall dwell in thy heart, O Lord? Oh! let me be one.

### JUNE 24TH.

#### THE SACRED HEART OF JESUS ZEALOUS.
#### FOR SOULS.

*Protectors,*—The Holy Angels of all those employed in gaining souls to Jesus, and St. John the Baptist.

### Practice.

Offer all your interior and exterior sufferings for the conversion of sinners. Be generous this day in honouring and imitating the zeal of the Heart of Jesus. Do what you can for the instruction of the ignorant, and to prevent the commission of sin. "Too happy should I be (said St. Ignatius), if by all my labors I prevented the commission of one sin."

### Aspiration.

Sacred Heart of Jesus, zealous for souls, have mercy on all poor sinners.

### JUNE 25TH.

#### THE SACRED HEART OF JESUS THE TENDER LOVER OF YOUTH.

*Protectors*,—The Archangels, and St. Philip Neri.

### Practice.

Honor, this day, and the 25th of every month, the sacred Heart of this Divine Infant Jesus. Think that he directly says to you, "Child, give me thy heart." Make an offering of your heart and affections, thrice, this day, to your Infant Saviour.

### Aspiration.

The Sacred Heart of the Infant Jesus, I love Thee.

## June 26th.

**THE SACRED HEART OF JESUS, THAT SO TENDERLY LOVED THE POOR AND SICK.**

*Protectors.*—The Holy Angels of all devoted to the service of the poor and sick, and Sts. Vincent of Paul and Catharine of Genoa.

### Practice.

With all the fervor of your soul, beg of the sacred Heart of Jesus, through the maternal Heart of Mary, the true spirit of charity. Relieve some poor person according to your means. Make an act of consecration.

### Aspiration.

Sacred Heart of Jesus, comfort of the afflicted, give me true charity. Health of the sick, pray for us.

## June 27th.

**THE SACRED HEART OF JESUS OUR PHYSICIAN.**

*Protectors.*—The Holy Angels especially devoted to the sacred Heart of Jesus, and St. Matilda.

### Practice.

Receive the sacred Heart of Jesus this day in the Holy Communion, at least spiritually, as the Physician of your soul. Confidently beg your cure. Ask pardon for having so often trusted in creatures rather than in the Hearts of Jesus and Mary. Make the Act of Consecration to the Sacred Heart.

### Aspiration.

Sacred Heart of Jesus, she "whom thou lovest is sick." Heart of Mary, health of the sick, pray for me.

### JUNE 28TH.

##### THE SACRED HEART OF JESUS OUR PEACE.

*Protectors,*—The Holy Angels of Peace, and St. Elizabeth of Hungary.

### Practice.

Say the "Gloria in Excelsis," in union with the Angels of Peace, begging of the Heart of Jesus, through the Heart of Mary, that peace promised to all of goodwill. Examine, before a picture of the sacred Heart, what has hitherto disturbed the peace of your soul.

### Aspiration.

Sacred Heart of Jesus, give me peace. Heart of Mary, pray for me.

### June 29th.

**THE SACRED HEART OF JESUS OUR JOY.**

*Protectors,*—The Archangels, and Sts. Peter and Paul.

### Practice.

Beg of the sacred Heart of Jesus to enlighten you, that you may see what are the usual subjects of your joy. See if they be like those of true children of God; if not, let this be the time for reparation. Say the hymn of the Holy Spirit.

### Aspiration.

Heart of Jesus, joy of Angels, have mercy on me. Heart of Mary, cause of our joy, pray for me.

## June 30th.

**THE SACRED HEART OF MARY, THE FIRST DEVOTED TO THE SACRED HEART OF JESUS, AND OUR WAY INTO THE DIVINE HEART.**

*Protectors*,—The Angels who have especially protected us during this month, and St. Joseph.

### Practice.

Now you have come to the close of this month of benediction, this harvest of the spiritual year; what are your feelings, your resolutions, your remorses, your gratitude, and your love? Tell all to the Heart of Jesus, review your protestations of fidelity in the service of Jesus. Say the Litany of the Sacred Heart in atonement for all the faults of this month.

### Aspiration.

Sacred Hearts of Jesus and Mary, I give you my heart and soul.

**OFFERING TO BE MADE THE LAST DAY OF THE MONTH.**

O sacred Heart of Jesus, I adore thee!

**I love thee!** I thank thee for all the favors I have received from thee during the past month and the whole course of my life. O divine Saviour! penetrated with sorrow at the sight of my sins, I detest them with all my heart for thy love. I conjure thee to receive me into thy sacred Heart and accept the donation I now make thee of all that I am. Receive this offering of my heart and all its affections. Amen.

# Visit to the Blessed Sacrament.

**FROM THE "VISITS" OF ST. LIGUORI.**

Faith teaches, and we are bound to believe that Jesus Christ is really present in the consecrated Host, under the appearance of bread. But we must know also that he remains on our altars, as on the throne of love and mercy, there to dispense his graces to us, and to show his love. He remains with us night and day, in this hidden manner, that Christians may visit him in the church, and by their devotions, their thanksgivings and affections, gratefully acknowledge and honor the loving presence of Jesus Christ, dwelling in the Sacrament of the altar. In the following devotions you will find many examples of the tender affection with which souls inflamed with the love of God, desired to remain in the presence of the most Holy Sacrament. You will find that all the saints have been enamored of this sweet devotion. On this earth we cannot find a more brilliant jewel, or a more lovely treasure, than Jesus in the Sacrament. Oh, how delightful it is to remain with faith, and with a tender devotion, at the foot of the altar, and to converse familiarly with Jesus Christ.

# If Thou Didst Believe.

## Behold I Am Always With You.

who dwells in our tabernacles for the purpose of hearing the prayers of all who visit him! How delightful to implore his pardon for our offences, to lay before him all our wants, as one friend does to another in whom he places all his confidence, to ask his grace, his love, and his glory! But O what a Paradise to continue in acts of love to that Lord, who remains on the altar interceding before his Father in our behalf, and burning with love for us! Blessed Henry Suso used to say that Jesus, on the altar, hears the prayers of the faithful more readily than he does in any other place. Make a trial of this devotion, and you will see the great fruit which you will gather from it. Be sure that of all the moments of your life, the time which you spend in devotion before this divine Sacrament will be that which shall give you the greatest support during life, and the greatest consolation at the hour of death, and for all eternity. And be persuaded that you will gain more in a quarter of an hour spent in prayer before the Holy Eucharist, than in all the other spiritual exercises of the day.

Do not, then, O devout soul, refuse to begin this devotion. From this day forward, retire each day from the conversation of men, and remain for some time, for a half-hour, or at least a quarter, in some church, before Jesus Christ in the Holy Sacrament.

**Prayer for the Visit to the Blessed Sacrament.**

Lord Jesus Christ, who, through the love which thou bearest to men, dost remain with them, day and night, in this sacrament, full of mercy and of love, expecting, inviting, and receiving all who come to visit thee; I believe that thou art present in the sacrament of the altar. From the abyss of my nothingness I adore thee, and I thank thee for all the favors which thou hast bestowed upon me, particularly for having given me thyself in this sacrament, for having given me for my advocate thy most holy mother, Mary, and for having called me to visit thee in this church.

I, this day, salute thy most loving heart, and I wish to salute it for three ends: first, in thanksgiving for this great gift; secondly, in compensation for all the injuries thou hast received from thy enemies, in this sacrament; thirdly, I wish, by this visit, to adore thee in all places in which thou art least honored and most abandoned in the holy sacrament. My Jesus, I love thee with my whole heart. I am sorry for having hitherto offended thy infinite goodness. I purpose, with the assistance of thy grace, never more to offend thee: and at this moment, miserable as I am, I consecrate my whole being to thee. I give thee my entire will, all my affections and desires, and all that I have. From this day forward do what thou wilt with me, and with whatever belongs to me. I ask and desire only thy holy love, the gift of final perseverance, and the perfect accomplishment of thy will. I recommend to thee the souls in purgatory, particularly those who were most devoted to the blessed sacrament and to most holy Mary; and I also recommend to thee all poor sinners. Finally, my dear Saviour, I unite all my affections with the affections of thy most loving heart; and, thus united, I offer them to thy eternal Father, and I entreat him, in

Thy name, and for Thy sake, to accept them.

100 days' indulgence. Plenary indulgence once a month.

### Prayer to the Blessed Sacrament.

Look down, O Lord! from Thy sanctuary, and from heaven, Thy dwelling place, and behold this holy Victim, which Thy holy Child, Jesus, our Lord, and great High Priest, offers up to Thee for the sins of his brethren; and let not Thy wrath be kindled upon us for the multitude of our transgressions. Behold, the voice of the blood of Jesus, our brother, calls to thee from the cross. Give ear, O Lord! Be appeased, O Lord! Hearken and do; and tarry not, for Thine own sake, O my God! because Thy name is called upon this city and upon Thy people; but deal with us according to Thy great mercy. Amen.

An indulgence of 100 days on any day. Plenary indulgence on the first Thursday of the month, if said on that day, after communion, and after fulfilling the ordinary conditions. Pius VI.

### Act of Reparation.

Jesus, my God, my Saviour, with that lowly homage with which the faith itself inspires me, I worship thee, very God and very Man; with my whole heart I love thee, enclosed in the most awful Sacrament of the Altar, in reparation for all the acts of irreverence, profanation, and sacrilege, which I may ever have been so unhappy as to have committed, as well as for all such like acts that ever have been done, or (which may God avert) ever may be done in ages yet to come. I adore thee, my God, not indeed according to the measure of thy merits, nor according to the greatness of my debt to thee, but according to the little strength I have; and fain would I adore thee with all the perfection of every reasonable creature. Meantime I purpose now and ever to adore thee, not only for those Catholics who adore thee not and love thee not, but also in the stead of, and for the conversion of, all heretics, schismatics, impious atheists, blasphemers, sorcerers, Turks, Jews, and idolaters. Jesus, my God, mayest thou be ever known, adored, loved and praised every moment, every day, in the most holy and most heavenly sacrament. Amen.

300 days indulgence.   Pius VII.

---

### Ejaculations.

I adore thee every moment, O living Bread of Heaven, great Sacrament!

Jesus, Heart of Mary, I pray thee send thy blessing on my soul.

Holiest Jesus! loving Saviour! I give thee all my heart.

May all know, adore, and praise every moment, always, the most divine Sacrament.

100 days indulgence.   Pope Leo XII.

O Sacrament most holy! O Sacrament divine!

All praise and all thanksgiving be every moment thine.

100 days indulgence.   Pius VI.

## The Devotion of the "Quarant Ore," or Forty Hours.

This devotion continues for forty hours, in memory of the forty hours during which the body of our Lord remained in the sepulchre. It was begun at Milan in 1524, was introduced into Rome by St. Philip Neri in 1548, and sanctioned by Pope Clement VIII., who issued a solemn Bull respecting it, November 25th, 1592.

This devotion owes its origin to Father Joseph, a Capuchin friar at Milan. In the year 1534, the city of Milan was suffering all the miseries attendant on war, and was reduced almost to despair, when Father Joseph called upon the citizens to raise their eyes from the miseries around them, and look up to heaven for succor, assuring them, on the part of God, that if they would give themselves to fervent prayer for forty hours, their city and their country would be liberated from the devastations of their enemies. The citizens obeyed the call. The Forty Hours Prayer commenced in the cathedral, and was taken up by the other churches of the city in rotation. The people meanwhile attended with fervor at the appointed prayers, and approached with great devotion the Sacraments of Penance and Holy Communion. Heaven did not delay to fulfil the assurance given by the pious servant of God; for in a short time the Emperor Charles V., and Francis, King of France, were seen at the gate of Milan arranging the articles of peace.

The prayer of the Forty Hours was established forever by Pope Clement VIII., for the whole course of the year, in regular continuous succession, from one church to another, commencing on the first Sunday in Advent. This pope was moved to establish this devotion by the public troubles of Holy Church, in order that, day and night, the faithful might appease their Lord by prayer, before the Blessed Sacrament in solemn exposition. The Indulgences are: A Plenary Indulgence to all who, after Confession and Communion, shall devoutly visit any church and pray there for the intention of the pope. An Indulgence of Ten Years and as many Quarantines for every visit made with contrition and a purpose of going to Confession. This Indulgence was confirmed by His Holiness, Pope Pius IX., by rescript, Nov. 26, 1876. By a rescript, May 10, 1807, Pius VII. declared further, that, henceforth and forever, in the churches where the Blessed Sacrament is exposed, all the altars are privileged during the time of the exposition.

## Praises to His Holy Name.

For the love we owe to God, and for the honor of his most holy name the following devout act of praise is to be said by way of reparation for the grievous offences which are committed against him by blasphemies; and in order that all the faithful may be incited to say them with devotion for every time that they are said with a contrite heart Pope Pius VII. granted—

One year's Indulgence.

His Holiness our Sovereign Lord Pius IX. grants likewise in addition to the above—

A Plenary Indulgence once a month to all those who at least once a day recite the said act of praise, provided that being truly contrite they Confess and Communicate, and visit some church or public oratory and pray there according to the mind of his holiness.

## The Act of Praise.

Blessed be God.
Blessed be His holy name.
Blessed be Jesus Christ, true God and true Man.
Blessed be the name of Jesus.
Blessed be Jesus in the most Holy Sacrament of the Altar.
Blessed be the great Mother of God Mary most holy.

Blessed be her holy and Immaculate Conception.

Blessed be the name of Mary, Virgin, and Mother.

Blessed be God in His holy angels and in His saints.

---

### Prayers and Petitions.

Indulgence of 300 days, once a day.

Plenary Indulgence to any one who shall recite them every day for a month on any one of the three last days of the month when, after Confession and Communion, he shall visit some church or public oratory, and pray according to the intention of the Sovereign Pontiff.

#### THE PRAYERS AND PETITIONS.

O Father! O Son! O Holy Ghost! O Holy Trinity! O Jesus! O Mary! O ye blessed Angels of God!

O all ye Saints of Paradise, men and women, obtain for me these graces, which I ask through the precious blood of Jesus Christ:

1. Ever to do the Holy will of God.
2. Ever to live in union with God.

3. Never to think of any one but God.

4. To love God alone.

5. To do all for God.

6. To seek alone God's glory.

7. To sanctify myself for God alone.

8. To know well my own utter nothingness.

9. Ever to know more and more the Will of my God.

10.   *   *   *   *   *   *

Mary most holy, offer to the Eternal Father the most Precious Blood of Jesus Christ for my poor soul, for the holy souls in purgatory, for the wants of Holy Church, for the conversion of sinners, for all the world.

Then say three Our Fathers, in honor of the most holy Blood of Jesus Christ, one Hail Mary, in honor of the sorrows of Mary most holy; and one " Requiem æternum " etc in behalf of the holy souls in purgatory.

## Prayer to Jesus Crucified.

"They pierced my hands and my feet; they numbered all my bones."—Ps. xxi. 17, 18.

For kissing a crucifix devoutly, one year's Indulgence each time.

A Plenary Indulgence, applicable to the souls in purgatory, can be gained, after confession and communion, by reciting this prayer before a crucifix, and praying for the intention of the Church.—Pius VII.

Look down upon me, good and gentle Jesus, while before thy face I humbly kneel, and with burning soul, pray and beseech thee to fix deep in my heart lively sentiments of faith, hope, and charity, true contrition for my sins, and firm purpose of amendment; that while I contemplate with great love and tender pity thy five wounds, pondering over them within me, whilst I call to mind the words which David, thy prophet, said of thee, my Jesus: "Foderunt manus Meas et pedes, Meos: dinumeraverunt omnia ossa Mea." "They pierced my hands and my feet; they numbered all my bones."—*Ps.* xxi. 17, 18.

### To Jesus Crucified.

O Lord Jesus! by that bitterness which Thou didst suffer for me on the Cross, chiefly when thy blessed soul was separated from thy body, have mercy on my soul now and at its departure from this world, that it may be admitted to life everlasting. Amen.

# On Devotion to the Blessed Virgin.

It is the opinion of St. Bernard, and of the generality of the theologians, that God gives no grace to man that does not pass through the hands of Mary. Hence, Suarez asserts that it is the sentiment of the Universal Church, that, to obtain God's graces, the intercession of Mary is not only useful, but even necessary. "Do you hope," asks St. Bernard, "to escape the horrors of spiritual shipwreck? Look on Mary, the bright star of the sea. In temptations, in all perplexities, call on Mary. Let her holy name ever hover on your lips; let it be deeply engraven on your heart. You cannot go astray while following her guidance: you cannot sink in despair while permitted to invoke her aid, you cannot fall while supported by her strength: you need not fear while shielded by her patronage. If she advocate your cause, you cannot fail to reach the haven of eternal peace." Mary is an advocate as merciful as she is powerful. Hence St. Bernard exhorts us to recommend ourselves with great confidence in all our necessities to this powerful advocate, who is all sweetness and benignity to those who invoke

J. SCHAEFER, PRINTER, 60 BARCLAY ST., N Y.

her intercession. "O God," exclaims St. Liguori, "how great shall be the remorse of the damned Christian in thinking that during life he could have saved his soul with so much facility by invoking the intercession of this Mother of mercy; that he had not done so: and that there shall be no more time to do it!" "Perhaps," says St. Bonaventure, "we are in doubt whether Mary will hear us when we address our prayers to her. No; Mary does not refuse, and never has refused, pity and aid to any sinner who has invoked her intercession." "Thou art the queen of mercy," says St. Bernard, "and who but the miserable are subjects of mercy? Devotion to the Blessed Virgin is an assured mark of predestination, for Mary is all-powerful with her divine Son." "The prayer of the divine Mother," says St. Antonine, "partakes of the nature of a command, and therefore it is impossible for her not to be heard."

Ah! let us never cease to have recourse in all our necessities to the divine mother, who is always ready to obtain relief for all who pray to her. But let us remember that devotion to the Mother of God, if real, must necessarily be practical. The holy fathers tell us, that in vain we flatter ourselves we love the Son, if we do not love the Mother; and that these two sentiments cannot be separated. They consider the love and devotion to Mary as one of the most precious gifts of grace, and the surest mark of predestination. But shall not the love of Mary for us inspire us also with love for her? she studies our wants, feels our afflictions, anticipates our requests, bears with our defects, and forgets our ingratitude. What, therefore, ought to be our eagerness to return her love for love! Let us, then, avail ourselves of every opportunity to honor her. Let us make it an inviolable rule daily to offer some prayers, to perform some good works, and to practise some virtues in her honor. Let us often visit an altar or image dedicated to her honor. Let us never pass a day without saying, *at least*, two decades of the Rosary, reciting the Angelus, and practising some acts of mortification in her honor. Let us endeavor to acquire the holy habit of frequently invoking her sacred name, especially in time of temptation; for St. Liguori says that we may disperse a legion of evil spirits by calling on the names of Jesus and Mary with faith and confidence.

Cultivate carefully, then, in your heart, devotion to the blessed Mother of God, and be sure that Mary will obtain for you great graces in return for the little acts of love and homage which you offer to her. In particular, do not neglect those devotions which are so well approved, and so generally practised by devout Catholics, such as the visits to the Blessed Virgin, the Litany, and the Rosary.

## Month of Mary.

The devotion of the Month of Mary consists in making the whole of May—the most charming month of the year—a continuous feast of thirty-one days in honor of the Queen of Heaven. It is productive of numerous graces and benedictions. The chief elements of the devotion are, the rich decoration of the sanctuaries, altars, and images of our Blessed Lady; the brilliant lights, which increase day after day, from the commencement to the solemn close of the month; the pious canticles harmonized and chanted, or, at least, repeated, by all the faithful: a short instruction or lecture, interspersed with some historic traits or facts, whose principal aim is to have us know, love, serve, invoke, and imitate holy Mary; prayers for the spiritual and temporal wants of the people; and, lastly, Benediction of the Blessed Sacrament, when the exercise takes place in a church, with a parting anthem in praise of the Immaculate

Virgin, whom they had assembled to venerate, extol, praise, and supplicate.

Pius VII., June 18, 1822, granted AN INDULGENCE OF 100 DAYS, once a day, to those who honor the Blessed Virgin by some devout exercise.

A PLENARY INDULGENCE, once during the month, after confession and communion, and prayer for the intention of the Sovereign Pontiff.

## "MEMORARE" OF ST. BERNARD TO THE BLESSED VIRGIN.

Remember, O most gracious Virgin Mary, that never was it known that any one who fled to thy protection, implored thy help, and sought thy intercession, was left unaided. Inspired with this confidence, I fly unto thee, O Virgin of virgins, my mother! To thee I come; before thee I stand, sinful and sorrowful. O mother of the Word incarnate! despise not my petitions, but, in thy mercy, hear and answer me. Amen.

His Holiness, Pius IX., July 25, 1846, granted every time this prayer is said:

AN INDULGENCE OF 300 DAYS.

A PLENARY INDULGENCE, once a month, to those who say it at least once a day for a month, on any one day after confession and communion, and prayer for the intention of the Sovereign Pontiff.

### Prayer before an Image or Picture of the B. V. M.

Most holy and immaculate Virgin! O my Mother! thou who art the Mother of my Lord, the Queen of the World, the advocate, hope and refuge of sinners! I, the most wretched among them, now come to thee. I worship thee, great Queen, and give thee thanks for the many favors thou hast bestowed on me in the past; most of all do I thank thee for having saved me from hell, which I had so often deserved. I love thee, lady most worthy of all love, and, by the love which I bear thee, I promise ever in the future to serve thee, and to do what in me lies to win others to thy love. In thee I put all my trust, all my hope of salvation. Receive me as thy servant, and cover me with the mantle of thy protection, thou who art the mother of mercy! And since thou hast so much power with God, deliver me from all temptations, or at least obtain for me the grace ever to overcome them. From thee I ask a true love of

Jesus Christ, and the grace of a happy death. O my mother! by thy love for God, I beseech thee to be at all times my helper, but, above all, at the last moment of my life. Leave me not until you see me safe in heaven, there for endless ages to bless thee and sing thy praises. Amen.

His Holiness, Pius IX., Sept. 7, 1854, granted to all who shall say this prayer before an image or picture of the Blessed Virgin, AN INDULGENCE OF 300 DAYS.

A PLENARY INDULGENCE, once a month, to all those who have said it every day for a month.

### OFFERING OR THE HEART OF JESUS TO THE BLESSED VIRGIN.

I praise and greet thee, O Virgin surpassingly sweet, in that intimate union wherewith thou art united to God above all creatures. And in amends, for all the negligences I have committed in thy service, I offer thee, O tender Mother, the most glorious and adorable Heart of Jesus Christ, with all that true and faithful filial love he showed thee in such perfection on earth, and will for ever show thee in heaven. Amen.

## Salve Regina.
### *At Morn.*

Hail, holy queen, mother of mercy, our life, our sweetness, and our hope; to thee do we cry, poor banished sons of Eve, to thee do we send up our sighs, mourning and weeping in this valley of tears. Turn, then, most gracious advocate, thine eyes of mercy toward us, and after this, our exile, show unto us the blessed fruit of thy womb, Jesus. O clement, O loving, O sweet Virgin Mary!

*V.* Make me worthy to praise thee, holy Virgin.

*R.* Give me strength against thine enemies.

*V.* Blessed be God in His saints.

*R.* Amen.

### *At Even.*

We fly to thy patronage, O holy Mother of God! despise not our petitions in our necessities, and deliver us from all dangers, O ever glorious and Blessed Virgin!

Make me worthy, etc.

Pius VI., April 5, 1786. granted an INDULGENCE of 100 DAYS, once a day, to all who shall say, with contrite heart and devotion, the *Salve Regina*, with the versicles, "Make worthy, etc." and "Blessed be God, etc." in the morning, and "We fly to thy patronage, etc.," with the same versicles in the evening.

AN INDULGENCE OF SEVEN YEARS AND SEVEN QUARANTINES on all the Sundays of the year.

A PLENARY INDULGENCE, twice a month, to all who shall recite these prayers as above directed : also, on all the feasts of the blessed Virgin Mary, as well as on the feast of All-saints, and at the hour of death, to all who have said them during life, on the above conditions.

---

PRAYER TO OUR LADY FOR PEACE.

Hail, august Queen of Peace! hail! holiest Mother of God! by the sacred heart of Jesus thy Son, the Prince of Peace, grant that his anger may end, and that in peace he may reign over us. Remember, O most loving Virgin Mary, that no one ever sought thy mediation without obtaining relief. Animated with this confidence, I come to thee. Do not, O Mother of the Word! despise my words, but hear and grant my prayer. O clement, O sweet Virgin Mary!

AN INDULGENCE OF 300 DAYS.—Pius IX., Sept. 23, 1846.

A PLENARY INDULGENCE to all who shall recite the above prayer once day, for a month, on usual conditions.

Google

"Go to Joseph and do all he will say to you."—GEN. chap. 41. v. 55.

"Beloved children, go to Joseph, and he will intercede for us in our distress."—Pius PP. IX.

J. SCHAEFER, PRINTER, 60 BARCLAY ST., N. Y.

# DEVOTION TO ST. JOSEPH.

St. Joseph is the patron of the Catholic Church, the high steward and the dispenser of the treasures of heaven. Do we wish to obtain any grace from God, let us by all means call on him. What is impossible in the ordinary course of Providence becomes easy through St. Joseph's intercession. For, how could our Lord refuse anything in heaven to him whom he wished to obey here on earth? The consideration that St. Joseph is as kind as he is powerful, will contribute to increase our confidence in him. As being the foster-father of the Son of God, the chaste Spouse of the Blessed Virgin Mary, and the Patron of the entire Church, he looks upon all its children as his own. Having treated our Lord with such paternal care, and the Blessed Virgin with such unvarying fidelity, could he ever refuse his help to those whom Mary tenderly loves, and for whom Jesus suffered and died?

Trust your soul to the fatherly care of St. Joseph, and ask every day from God the grace of a happy death, through the merits and intercession of him who had the happiness **of dying assisted by Jesus and Mary.**

## Month of March.

It is dedicated to St. Joseph, because the glorious Patriarch's principal feast is celebrated in that month. Thus, it serves as a preparation for, and, as it were, an introduction to the delightful month of May. From the Bridegroom we go to the Bride. In truth, Joseph is the way to Mary—*per Joseph ad Mariam.*

As in the case of that of Mary, the chief ingredients of the exercises peculiar to this blessed month are, a tasty decoration of his image or altar with flowers and lights, accompanied with prayers, canticles, sermons or lectures, or meditation on the worship of the saint, good works, &c.

Although the devotion is in existence only a few years, it has its beneficent branches already extended far and near. Wherefore, on our part let us try to do something to honor him, as, for instance to keep a lamp lighting each day of this month before his statue or picture.

This generous act of piety, besides carrying out the spirit of the Church, will be more than amply recompensed.

His Holiness Pius IX., June 11, 1855, granted, to all who shall dedicate the month of March to the honor of St. Joseph:

AN INDULGENCE OF THREE HUNDRED DAYS, for each day of the month.

A PLENARY INDULGENCE, on any one day of the month, after confession and communion.

## MEMORARE TO ST. JOSEPH.

Remember, O most pure spouse of the blessed Virgin Mary, my sweet protector, St. Joseph! that no one ever had recourse to thy protection, or implored thy aid without obtaining relief. Confiding therefore in thy goodness, I come before thee, and humbly supplicate thee. O, despise not my petitions, foster-father of the Redeemer, but graciously receive them. Amen.

An indulgence of three hundred days, once a day. Pope Pius IX., June 26, 1863.

### Choice of St. Joseph as a Patron.

O Blessed Joseph, faithful guardian of my Redeemer, Jesus Christ; protector of thy chaste spouse, the Virgin Mother of God; I choose thee this day to be my special patron and advocate, and I firmly resolve to honor thee from this time forth. Therefore I humbly beseech thee to receive me as thy client, to instruct me in every doubt, to comfort me in every affliction, to obtain for me and for all the knowledge and love of the Heart of Jesus, and finally to defend and protect me at the hour of death. Amen.

### For a Happy Death.

O Blessed Joseph, who didst yield thy last breath in the fond embrace of Jesus and of Mary—when the seal of death shall close my career of life, come, holy father, with Jesus and Mary, to aid me and obtain for me this only solace which I ask for in that hour, to die encircled by their holy arms. Into your sacred hands, living and dying, Jesus, Mary, Joseph, I commend my soul. Amen.

*V.* Pray for us, O most blessed Joseph.

*R.* That we may be made worthy of the promises of Christ.

---

### Ejaculatory Prayers to obtain a Good Death.

Jesus, Mary, and Joseph, I give you my heart and my soul.

Jesus, Mary, and Joseph, assist me in my last agony.

Jesus, Mary, and Joseph, my I breathe forth my soul in peace with you.

Pius VII., April 28, 1807, granted to all who, with at least contrite heart and devotion, shall say these three ejaculations:

An indulgence of three hundred days.

An indulgence of one hundred days, every time that, with the same dispositions, they shall say one of these ejaculations.

## Devotion of the Six Sundays in Honor of St. Aloysius Gonzaga.

In order to increase the fervor of the faithful, and especially of youth, in devotion to the angelic youth, Aloysius, Clement XII., by two decrees of the S. Congregation of Indulgences, on the 11th December, 1739, and 7th January, 1740, grants a perpetual Plenary Indulgence on each of the Six Sundays that are celebrated in honor of the Saint, either before his feast (21st June), or at any other time during the year. To gain these indulgences it is required that the said Six Sundays should be consecutive, not interrupted, and that on each the faithful should, after confession and communion, devote some time to pious meditations or vocal prayers, or to some other works of Christian piety in honor of the Saint.

1st Sunday, St. Aloysius, model of compunction of heart.

2d Sunday, St. Aloysius, model of obedience.

3d Sunday, St. Aloysius, model of purity.

4th Sunday, St. Aloysius, model of love of God.

5th Sunday, St. Aloysius, model of devotion to the Blessed Virgin.

6th Sunday, St. Aloysius, model of zeal for salvation of souls.

Each Sunday recite, six times, Our Father, Hail Mary, and Glory be to the Father, as well to gain the holy indulgence as to obtain from Jesus, through the intercession of

Mary, the imitation of the six virtues of St. Aloysius, on which we meditate during this devotion.

## PRAYER TO ST. ALOYSIUS.

O Blessed Aloysius, adorned with angelic graces, I, thy most unworthy suppliant, recommend specially to thee the chastity of my soul and body, praying thee by thy angelic purity to plead for me with Jesus Christ, the Immaculate Lamb, and his Holy Mother, Virgin of virgins, that they would vouchsafe to keep me from all grievous sin. O never let me be defiled with any stain of fleshly sin, but when thou dost see me in temptation, or in danger of falling, then far from my heart remove all bad thoughts and unclean desires, and awaken in me the memory of eternity to come and Jesus crucified: impress deeply in my heart a sense of the holy fear of God; and thus kindling in me the fire of divine love, enable me so to follow thy footsteps here on earth, that in heaven with thee I may be made worthy to enjoy the vision of our God forever. Amen.

Our Father, * * * Hail Mary.

Pius VII., granted an indulgence of 100 days to all who say the above prayer devoutly, with one Our Father and one Hail Mary.

# DEVOTION TO THE ANGELS.

"*Are they not all ministering spirits, sent to minister for them who shall receive the inheritance of salvation?*"—Heb. i. 14.

"The Angels," says St. Augustine, "love us as their fellow-citizens, and hope to see us fill up what has been lost to their own number by the fall of the rebel angels. For this reason they are always present with us, and watch over us with the greatest care. At all times, and in every place, they are ready to help us, and to provide for our wants. They walk with us in all our ways: going out and coming in, they follow us still, anxiously considering whether we live piously and purely in the midst of a wicked world. They assist those who labor; they guard those who rest; they encourage those who fight; they crown those who conquer; they rejoice with the joyful, and sympathize with the suffering. When we do well, the angels are glad, but the devils are sad. When we sin the devils rejoice, but the angels are cheated of their joy." (Solil. cap. 27.)

We ought, therefore, to honor these blessed spirits with very great reverence and affection, and to pray to them, especially our guardian angels, to whom God has given charge over us, to keep us in all our ways (Ps. xc.), and we may be sure that this devotion will be most pleasing to them, and most useful to ourselves.

Celestial guardian thus with thee—
And by thy constant care,
May I the world's corruption flee
And heavenly blessings share.

Google

### Prayer to the Guardian Angel.

O blessed angel, my guardian and defender, since by the kind providence of God I have been committed to thy care, I beseech thee to direct me always in the way of peace, safety, and salvation. Defend me from all danger and temptation. Remember, O dearest guardian, that the grace of God preserved thee, with the good angels in heaven, when the proud ones were cast into hell. I beseech thee, therefore, to assist me so efficaciously, that in this life of trial I may never be overcome by any temptation; that I may love and serve my God faithfully, and that I may die in the grace of God. Amen.

---

An indulgence of 100 days each time the following hymn is said with devotion in honor of the Guardian Angel, and if said daily, a Plenary indulgence once a month.—Pius VI.

Angel of God, my guardian dear,
To whom his love commits me here,
Ever this day be at my side,
To light and guard, to rule and guide.
Amen.

## Devotion to the Souls in Purgatory.
### (by st. alphonsus liguori.)

The practice of recommending to God the souls in purgatory, that he may mitigate the great pains which they suffer, and that he may soon bring them to his glory, is most pleasing to the Lord, and most profitable to us. For these blessed souls are his eternal spouses, and most grateful are they to those who obtain their deliverance from prison, or even a mitigation of their torments. When, therefore, they arrive in heaven, they will be sure to remember all who have prayed for them. It is a pious belief that God manifests to them our prayers in their behalf, that they also may pray for us. It is true, these blessed souls are not in a state to pray for themselves, because they are, so to speak, criminals atoning for their faults. However, because they are very dear to God, they can pray for us, and obtain for us the divine graces. St. Catharine of Bologna, when she wished to obtain any grace, had recourse to the souls in purgatory, and her prayers were heard immediately. She declared that, by praying to those holy souls, she obtained many favors which she had sought through the intercession of the saints without obtaining them. The graces which devout persons are said to have received through these holy souls are innumerable.

But, if we wish for the aid of their prayers, it is just, it is even a duty, to relieve them by our suffrages. I say, *it is even a duty:* for Christian charity commands us to relieve our neighbors who stand in need of our assistance. But who among all our neighbors have so great need of our help as these holy prisoners? They are continually in that fire which torments more severely than any earthly fire. They are deprived of the sight of God, a torment far more excruciating than all other pains. Let us reflect that among these suffering souls are parents, or brothers, or relations and friends, who look to us for succor. Let us remember, moreover, that, being in the condition of debtors for their sins, they cannot assist themselves. This thought should urge us forward to relieve them to the best of our ability. By assisting them we shall not only give great pleasure to God, but will acquire also great merit for ourselves. And in return for our suffrages, these blessed souls will not neglect to obtain for us many graces from God, but particularly the grace of eternal life. I hold for certain that a soul delivered from Purgatory by the suffrages of a Christian, when she enters Paradise, will not fail to say to God: "Lord do not suffer to be lost that person who has liberated me from the prison of Purgatory, and has brought me to the enjoyment of thy glory sooner than I had deserved!"

St. Liguori then goes on to urge the faithful to do all in their power to relieve and liberate these blessed souls, by procuring masses to be said for them, by alms, and by their own fervent prayers.

*Prayers for the Souls in Purgatory.*

O dearest Jesus, by the bloody sweat which thou didst suffer in the Garden of Gethsemani, have mercy on these blessed souls.

*R.* Have mercy on them, O Lord, have mercy on them.

O dearest Jesus, by the pains which thou didst suffer during thy most cruel scourging, have mercy on them.

*R.* Have mercy on them, &c.

O dearest Jesus, by the pains which thou didst suffer from thy most painful crown of thorns, have mercy on them.

*R.* Have mercy on them, &c.

O dearest Jesus, by the pains which thou didst suffer in carrying thy cross to Calvary, have mercy on them.

*R.* Have mercy on them, &c.

O dearest Jesus, by the pains which thou didst suffer in thy most cruel crucifixion, have mercy on them.

*R.* Have mercy on them, &c.

O dearest Jesus, by the pains which thou didst suffer in thy most bitter agony on the cross, have mercy on them.

*R.* Have mercy on them, &c.

O dearest Jesus, by that intense pain which thou didst suffer in breathing forth thy blessed soul, have mercy on them.

*R* Have mercy on them, &c.

---

*Psalm, De profundis.*

Out of the depths I have cried to thee, O Lord; Lord, hear my voice.

Let thy ears be attentive to the voice of my supplication.

If thou, O Lord, will mark iniquities, Lord, who shall stand it?

For with thee there is merciful forgiveness; and by reason of thy law I have waited for thee, O Lord.

My soul hath relied on his word; my soul hath hoped in the Lord.

From the morning watch even until night, let Israel hope in the Lord.

Because with the Lord there is mercy, and with him plentiful redemption.

And he shall redeem Israel from all his iniquities.

Glory be, &c.

*V.* Give them eternal rest, O Lord.

*R.* And let perpetual light shine on them.

*V.* May they rest in peace.

*R.* Amen.

### *Prayer.*

O God, the author of mercy and lover of the salvation of mankind, we address thy clemency in behalf of our brethren, relations, and benefactors who are departed this life, that by the intercession of blessed Mary ever Virgin, and of all the saints, thou wouldst receive them into the enjoyment of eternal happiness; through Christ our Lord. Amen.

Now recommend yourselves to the souls in Purgatory, and say:

Blessed souls! we have prayed for you. We entreat you, who are so dear to God, and so sure of never losing him, to pray for us miserable sinners, who are in danger of being damned, and of losing God forever.

---

## Prayers for the Whole Week.

Pope Leo XII., in order to hold out a greater inducement to the faithful to aid the departed, granted, by a Rescript of the S. Congr. of Indulgences, Nov. 18, 1826—

The Indulgence of 100 days, once a day to all who say the following prayers, each day in the week, with one Our Father, Hail Mary, and the *De profundis*.

### *For Sunday.*

O Lord God Almighty, I pray thee, by the precious blood which thy divine Son Jesus shed in the garden, deliver the souls in purgatory, and specially amongst them all, that soul which is most destitute of aid; and bring it to thy glory, there to praise and bless thee forever. Amen.

*Our Father, Hail Mary, De profundis.*

### For Monday.

O Lord God Almighty, I pray thee, by the precious blood which thy divine Son Jesus shed in his cruel scourging, deliver the souls in purgatory, and amongst them all that soul specially which is nearest to its entrance into thy glory; that so it may soon begin to praise and bless thee forever. Amen.

*Our Father, Hail Mary, De profundis.*

### For Tuesday.

O Lord God Almighty, I pray thee, by the precious blood which thy divine Jesus shed in his bitter crowning with thorns, deliver the souls in purgatory, and in particular amongst them all, deliver that one which would be the last to issue out of those pains, that it tarry not so long a time before it come to praise thee in thy glory and bless thee forever. Amen.

*Our Father, Hail Mary, De profundis.*

### For Wednesday.

O Lord God Almighty, I pray thee by the precious blood which thy divine Son Jesus shed through the streets of Jerusalem when he carried the cross upon his sacred shoulders, deliver the souls in purgatory, and specially that soul which is richest in merits before thee; that so, in that throne of glory which awaits it, it may magnify thee and bless thee forever. Amen.

*Our Father, Hail Mary, De profundis.*

### For Thursday.

O Lord God Almighty, I beseech thee, by the precious body and blood of thy divine Son Jesus, which he gave with his own hand upon the eve of his passion to his beloved apostles to be their meat and drink, and which he left to his whole Church to be a perpetual sacrifice and life-giving food of his own faithful people, deliver the souls in purgatory, and specially that one which was most devoted to this mystery of infinite love; that with thy same divine Son, and with thy Holy Spirit, it may ever praise thee for this thy wondrous love in thy eternal glory. Amen.

*Our Father, Hail Mary, De profundis.*

### For Friday.

O Lord God Almighty, I pray thee, by the precious blood which thy divine Son shed on this day upon the wood of the cross from his most sacred hands and feet, deliver the souls in purgatory, and specially that soul for which I am bound to pray; that the blame rest not with me that thou bringest it not forthwith to praise thee in thy glory and to bless thee forever. Amen.

*Our Father, Hail Mary, De profundis.*

## THE SOULS IN PURGATORY.

*For Saturday.*

O Lord God Almighty, I beseech thee, by the precious blood which burst forth from the side of thy divine Son Jesus, in the sight of, and to the extreme pain of, his most holy Mother, deliver the souls in purgatory, and specially that one amongst them all which was ever the most devout to this great Lady; that it may soon attain unto thy glory, there to praise thee in her and her in thee, world without end. Amen.

*Our Father, Hail Mary, De profundis*

## Prayers at Mass

### IN UNION WITH THE SACRED HEART OF JESUS.

How agreeable must it not be to the loving Heart of our divine Lord to have us unite our petitions with those that he presented to his eternal Father, when he offered himself up on Calvary for our salvation.

It is then a praiseworthy custom to offer up our prayers during the holy sacrifice of the Mass in union with the sacred Heart of Jesus. These prayers will be most acceptably received at the throne of grace and mercy.

#### DIRECT YOUR INTENTION.

I offer thee, O my God, this august sacrifice, to honor thy unspeakable perfections, to thank thee for all the graces which thou hast so often heaped upon me, to ask thy pardon for my numberless infidelities, and to obtain of thee new favors.

O Jesus, grant me, I beseech thee, a constant attention, a profound reverence, a lively faith, and a tender devotion during the adorable sacrifice; set me on fire with the love of thee, that I may partake of the merits which thou hast obtained for me at the price of thy most precious blood.

## THE SACRED HEART OF JESUS.

### AT THE INTROIBO.

O divine Jesus, thou art the victim laden with all the iniquities of the world: thou didst shed bitter tears for them; thou didst expiate them by the most dreadful torments and by the most cruel of deaths. I come to mingle my tears with thine; I confess to thee, in the presence of Mary, ever Virgin, and of all the saints, that I have sinned exceedingly; that it is my ingratitude that pierced thy heart, and put thee to a cruel death. O God, my Saviour, through thy tears, through thy agony in the Garden of Olives, through thy precious blood and the wound in thy sacred Heart, I beseech thee to pardon me, and to grant me the remission of all my sins.

### THE INTROIT.

Let us adore the Heart of Jesus, which has loved us so much; let us prostrate ourselves before him, and bewail the sins of which we have been guilty. Grant us, O Lord, a contrite and humble heart; let the homage of our adorations be as acceptable to thee as if we offered thee thousands of victims.

### THE KYRIE.

O Father of infinite mercy, have pity on thy children; O Jesus immolated for us, apply to us the merits of thy precious blood; O Holy Ghost the Sanctifier, descend into our hearts, and inflame them with thy love.

### THE GLORIA.

What happiness for us that the Son of the Most High should have been pleased to dwell among us, and have vouchsafed to offer us a dwelling in his divine Heart! Suffer us, O Lord, to mingle our voices with those of the angelic choir, to thank thee for so great a favor; and to unite with them in saying: Glory to God in the highest heavens. O almighty Father, we praise thee, we bless thee, we adore thee, we give thee thanks for all the benefits which thou hast lavished upon us without ceasing. O Jesus, Lamb without spot, who takest away the sins of the world, have mercy on us; thou only art holy, thou only art the Lord, who reignest with the Father and the Holy Ghost in glory everlasting.

### THE COLLECTS.

O Divine Jesus, inexhaustible fountain of all good things, open unto us, we beseech thee, the interior of thy Heart; that, having entered by pious meditation into this august sanctuary of divine love, we may fix forever there our hearts, as the place wherein are found the treasure, rest and happiness of holy souls; who livest and reignest forever and ever.

### THE EPISTLE.

"He shall grow up as a tender plant before the Lord, and as a root out of a thirsty ground: there is no beauty in him nor comeliness: and we have seen him, and there was no sightliness, that we should be desirous of him: despised, and the most abject of men, a man of sorrows, and acquainted with infirmity:

and his look was as it were hidden and despised; whereupon we esteemed him not. Surely he hath borne our infirmities, and carried our sorrows: and we have thought him as it were a leper, and as one struck by God and afflicted. But he was wounded for our iniquities, he was bruised for our sins: the chastisement of our peace was upon him, and by his bruises we are healed. All we like sheep have gone astray, every one hath turned aside into his own way: and the Lord hath laid on him the iniquity of us all. He was offered because it was his own will, and he opened not his mouth: he shall be led as a sheep to the slaughter, and shall be dumb as a lamb before his shearer, and he shall not open his mouth. He was taken away from distress, and from judgment: who shall declare his generation? because he is cut off out of the land of the living: for the wickedness of my people have I struck him." *Isaiah* liii., 2.

THE GRADUAL.

Let the tears flow from our eyes, day

and night, as a torrent; let our hearts be poured out like water before the Lord: let us raise up our hands to him.

Heart of Jesus, pardon thy children; let not thy heritage fall into reproach; save us, and we will never cease to sing thy mercies.

### THE GOSPEL.

O Lord Jesus, teach us what we must do to gain eternal life.

"My little children, I give you a new commandment: that you love one another; as I have loved you, that you also love one another. By this shall all men know that you are my disciples, if you have love one for another. If you love me, keep my commandments. And I will ask the Father, and he will give you the spirit of truth, whom the world knoweth not. I will not leave you orphans: I will come to you: you shall know that I am in my Father, and you in me, and I in you. He that keepeth my commandments, he it is that loveth me; and he that loveth me, shall be loved of my Father; and I will love him, and will open to him my **Heart**. Abide in me; if any one abide not in me, he shall be cast forth as a branch, and shall wither; and they shall cast him into the fire and he burneth. If you abide in me, and my words abide in you, you shall ask whatever you will, and it shall be done unto you. It is the will of my Father that you bring forth good fruit, and become my disciples. A little while, and you shall not see me; you shall lament and weep, but the world shall rejoice; but I will see you again, and your heart shall rejoice, and your joy no man shall take from you. In the world you shall have distress: but have confidence, I have overcome the world. Holy Father, keep them in thy name whom thou hast given me, that they may be one, as we also are. I pray not that thou shouldst take them out of the world, but that thou shouldst keep them from evil. Father, I will that where I am, they also whom thou hast given me may be with me, that they may see my glory. *St. John,* xiii–xvii.

### THE CREDO.

I believe, O my God, the truths which thou hast revealed to thy Church. I desire to live and die in this faith. Grant O Lord, that my life may be conformable to my faith; that my faith may be animated by good works; that I may never be ashamed to declare myself a Catholic, and may constantly maintain the interests of thy holy religion.

O holy Roman Catholic Church, the persecutions which thou hast endured, far from weakening my faith, do but strengthen it the more, since thy divine spouse foretold them. I vow inviolable attachment to thee. Lord, draw close the bonds that bind me to thy holy Church; put into my heart a spirit of perfect obedience to its lawful pastors. In its bosom I became thy child, and in its bosom I wish to live and die. Amen.

### THE OFFERTORY.

O Jesus, we draw near with confidence to thy sacred Heart; cast upon us, we beseech thee, a look of pity, and make our hearts a perpetual offering consecrated to our glory.

Sin made us the enemies of our God, but Jesus Christ, by his death, hath reconciled us with his divine Father. It is in the sacred Heart that this reconciliation is effected. O my soul, how Jesus Christ hath loved us! At what a price he hath redeemed us! Not with gold, nor with riches; but by the voluntary shedding of his blood. He hath sacrificed himself for us: let us then live only for him; let us sacrifice ourselves together with him.

Thou willest, O Jesus, that I become a victim of love, wholly consecrated to thy divine Heart: it is my most ardent desire. Thy benefits are numberless; thou hast broken the bonds of my servitude; thou hast adopted me for thy child; thou hast admitted me to thy table; thou hast given me a place in thy divine Heart; and even yet, despite my continual prevarications, thou preparest me an everlasting blessedness; how could I ever forget so many benefits! I will publish thy mercies, and will never cease to love thee with all the fervor of my heart. But, O my God, my heart is not full enough of love and fervor to be an offering worthy of thee. What, then, shall I give thee? I will give thee thy Son. That Son, the most worthy object of thy complacency, will supply my inability. O Lord, look not on me, but on this divine offering.

### THE PREFACE.

Lift up, O Lord, do thou thyself lift up, my heart to thee. Take from it all unholy thoughts, all earthly affections. Lift it wholly up to heaven, where thy Heart is worthily adored, and to the altar where it is about to manifest itself to me. My life is but one continual succession of thy mercies, let it be one continual succession of thanksgivings; and as thou art now about to renew the greatest of all sacrifices, is it not meet that I should burst forth in expressions of heartfelt gratitude? Suffer me then, to join my feeble voice with the voices of all the heavenly spirits, and in union with them to say, in transports of joy and admiration: Holy, holy, holy is the Heart of Jesus, the worthy object of the divine complacency, and of the homage of heaven and earth. The whole earth is full of its glory and its mercy; let my heart be full also of its love.

### THE CANON.

O God, infinitely holy, if my sins provoke thee, and make me abominable in thy sight, look upon the Lamb without spot, who is going to immolate himself to take away the sins of the world, and, beholding his merits, remember not my ingratitude. Remember only that I have been graciously admitted into the Heart of thy divine Son, and am intimately united to it. This Heart, infinitely merciful, prayed for me on Calvary, and will soon renew the sacrifice of itself for me.

O my God, would that I had all the sorrow which filled the Heart of Jesus, the man of sorrows, when, weighed down under the heavy burden of my sins, and ready to expiate them by cruel torments, he wept grievously in the Garden of Olives, and, all covered with bloody sweat, made for me an act of reparation to thy outraged Majesty, imploring thy mercy with deep sighs and groans! I earnestly desire this perfect sorrow. I confess that I have sinned exceedingly in offending thee, by repaying thy benefits with outrages and insults. There is nothing I would not do to expiate my innumerable sins; I would willingly shed my blood to satisfy thy justice.

### THE CONSECRATION.

But what do I behold upon the altar? Is it not that holy Victim which shall reconcile me to my God? O my soul, this bread will become the body of the Son of God, and this wine, his blood; and this most marvelous change will be wrought by one word. There needed but one word to create this vast universe; that same word will this day work the greatest of all wonders, and will renew it even to the end of the world. Mary, Mother of God, and all ye blessed spirits who surround the throne of the Most High, holy men and women, saints of God, come ye and witness this miracle of love, which is the pledge of my salvation.

O my soul, enter into thyself; believe that Jesus Christ is really present in the holy Eucharist. Yes, my God, this is thy body, this is thy blood: thou hast said it; I am silent before thee; I believe, I adore.

### AFTER THE CONSECRATION.

O Jesus, victim of thy love for me, touch my heart; communicate to me at this moment all the ardent affections of the saints who have loved thee with the deepest tenderness, and all the burning adorations of the seraphim, whose blessed privilege it is always to behold thee. Kindle in my heart the devouring fire that consumes thine own, that, animated with thy spirit, I may live a life altogether new. O my Saviour, thou standest ever before thy Father; thou showest him the marks of thy wounds and the opening in thy Heart; thou ever livest to make intercession for us. And dost thou not perform the same ministry upon this altar? Occupied wholly with my needs, thou layest them before thy Father; thou presentest thy Heart to him, to appease his anger and obtain his grace for me. O divine Lord, I lay all my petitions at thy feet; vouchsafe to present them to thy Father. I pray for the conversion of sinners, the perseverance of the just, and the triumph of our holy religion. O Jesus, who didst die for all men, bring back to the fold of thy Church those who are separated from it. Enlighten all infidels and heretics; bless the efforts of those who labor to convert them. Have pity on the souls of the faithful departed; remit to them their debts, and grant them a place of refreshment, light, and peace. I beseech thee particularly to have compassion on (*Name them*).

### THE PATER.

O my Father, if it be permitted that a guilty child call by so tender a name a God whom he hath so often offended, grant that I may ever labor for the glory of thy holy name, that in all things I may do thy will, and sigh unceasingly for thy heavenly kingdom. Feed me with the bread of heaven, with which thou feedest the beloved children of thy Heart. Let the forgiveness which thou didst grant thy murderers be my model in forgiving those who have injured me; give me superiors, both spiritual and temporal, that love thee, and friends that serve thee faithfully; and if ever I expose myself to sin, do thou deliver me from the danger, that I may never outrage thy divine Heart.

### THE AGNUS DEI.

Lamb of God, who takest away the sins of the world, have mercy on me. Give me the peace which the world cannot give: peace with thee, by a true reconciliation and a perfect submission to thy will; peace with myself, by the subjection of my passions; peace with my neighbor, by the union of a sincere charity with all the children of men. Give peace to the world, by the extinction of wars and divisions.

### THE COMMUNION.

*If you are to communicate, say:*

Is there any love to be compared with thine, my Saviour! It was on the cross that thou didst offer thy sacrifice, and it is in my heart that thou desirest to consummate it. O my God, is it possible that thou choosest for thy abode a heart so wretched? Alas, I am nothing but a sinner! Whence is it, Lord, that, despite all my unworthiness, thou desirest me to sit down at thy table? Since thus it is, speak but the word and my soul shall be healed; say to me, as thou didst say to the woman that was a sinner: Thy sins are forgiven. Make me hear the words which thou didst speak to Zaccheus: Make haste; for this day I must abide in thy house.

*If you are not to communicate, say:*

O my most loving Saviour, since I have not the happiness of receiving thee this day, suffer me to gather up the precious crumbs that fall from thy table, and to unite myself to thy divine Heart, by faith, hope, and charity. I confess I do not deserve thy children's bread; but I venture humbly to declare that, away from thee, my soul is dried up with thirst, and my heart cast down with faintness. Come then, O my divine Jesus! and take up thy abode within me. Come into my mind, and illuminate it with thy light; come into my heart, and enkindle in it the fire of thy love, and unite it so intimately with thy own, that it may be no longer I that live, but thou that livest in me, and reignest in me for ever.

### THE POST COMMUNION.

Learn of me, for I am meek and humble of heart, and you shall find rest to your souls: my yoke is sweet, and my burden light.

Lord, we have had the happiness of being admitted into the sanctuary of thy divine Heart, give us grace that we may abide therein forever; so that we may obtain the happiness which thou hast prepared for thy elect; through thy Son, our Lord Jesus Christ. Amen.

### THE BENEDICTION.

O Heart of Jesus, I will not depart till thou hast blessed me. Bless me in the name of the Father, and of the Son, and of the Holy Ghost; and let thy blessing descend upon all those for whom I ought to pray.

### THE LAST GOSPEL.

O eternal Word, who wast made man that thou mightest make men the children of God, I thank thee for this unspeakable grace. How great is the blessing I enjoy, not only of bearing the name, but of being indeed the child of God. Grant, O my Jesus, that I may preserve this blessed title, by faithfully imitating thy sacred Heart, and showing myself always filled with love for thy holy law.

If I remain faithful, thou assurest me that I shall be co-heir with thee, and shall enjoy the happiness which thou hast purchased for us with thy precious blood; and this I hope to obtain through thy infinite mercy.

### AFTER MASS.

How great will be my happiness, O Lord, if, by assisting at this divine sacrifice, I have received all the graces which thou grantest to those who bring thereto a lively faith and a pure heart. Accept, I beseech thee, the reparation which I offer thy divine majesty for all the sins of which I have been guilty before thy holy altar. I am going to occupy myself with those duties in the world to which thy providence hath called me. Grant that I may have before my mind thy patience in adversities, thy obedience to Joseph and Mary, and thy tender charity in bearing with all men. Strengthen me against all temptations; preserve me from all sin; make me firm and immovable in the faith; in fine, transform me into thyself, O Jesus, so that thy Heart and my heart may be united in one, both in time and in eternity. Amen.

## SCAPULAR OF THE SACRED HEART.

### A PRESERVATIVE AGAINST CONTAGIOUS DISEASES.

WHEN the terrible pestilence of 1720 was raging in Marseilles, and mowing down, day by day, its thousand and more victims, as was certified by the Bishop of that city himself, before the assembly of the clergy, there dwelt at Marseilles, in the odor of sanctity, a Nun of the Visitation, named Magdalen Remusat, a fervent worshipper of the Sacred Heart of Jesus. At her solicitation, the bishop, in order to avert the scourge, solemnly consecrated the whole city and diocese to the Sacred Heart of Jesus Christ, and so marvellous and prompt were the effects of this consecration, that all men held them to be miraculous. From that time forth, Sister Magdalen advised all to wear upon their breast, in the form of a scapular, as a preservative against infection, the image of the Sacred Heart of Jesus, with the inscription, "**Cease; the Heart of Jesus is with me.**"

The pious practice, which spread greatly by means of the Nuns of the Visitation, was of marvellous efficacy in all subsequent cases of contagion, as seen in 1866, in the city and diocese of Amiens, and in 1867, in Lombardy and various other parts of Italy.

This scapular consists of an image of the Sacred Heart mounted upon a square of white woollen, with the inscription:

"Cease; the Heart of Jesus is with me."

By a rescript of the 28th day of October, 1872, His Holiness, Pius IX., cordially granted an indulgence of 100 days to be gained every day by the Christian Faithful who wear the badge of the Sacred Heart, provided they recite some pious prayer, such as the *Our Father, Hail Mary, Glory be to the Father*, or the following:

"Open thy Sacred Heart to me, O most sweet Jesus! Manifest its charms to me; unite me to it forever. May all the aspirations and throbs of my heart, which beats unceasingly, even during sleep, be a pledge of my love, and repeat continually to Thee: I love Thee. Receive the little good I do, and grant me grace to atone for sin, so that I may praise Thee in time, and bless Thee in eternity. Amen.

## CONFRATERNITY OF THE MOST SACRED HEART OF JESUS.

The object of this Confraternity is to honor the Divine Heart of Jesus; to render him love for love; to thank him for all his mercies and favors, especially for the institution of the Blessed Eucharist; and to make him reparation for the coldness and ingratitude with which his infinite charity is repaid by the generality of Christians. "It is this I feel more than all I suffered in my Passion," our Lord said to the Blessed Margaret Mary Alacoque. "If men would only return my love, I would count all I have done for them as nothing; but, instead of that, I receive from them, for the most part, only coldness and ingratitude. Do thou, at least, atone for their ungratefulness as far as thou art able." The spirit of devotion to the Sacred Heart of Jesus may be gathered from these words of our Lord. It is two-fold: *First*, to make the love of that Sacred Heart for us the subject of frequent and affectionate meditation, and to aim at making a return of love for such infinite love. *Secondly*, to mourn over and to endeavor to make atonement for the many insults and outrages to which he was subjected during his mortal life, and which, unhappily, he still so frequently meets with, especially in the most holy Sacrament of the altar.

A special devotion to the Blessed Sacrament is intimately connected with that to the Sacred Heart: 1. Because such is the evident intention of our Blessed Lord as evidenced in the circumstances under which he instituted the devotion of the Sacred Heart. 2. Because the Sacred Heart of Jesus is really present, along with his soul and divinity, in the most holy sacrament. 3. Because his Sacramental Presence on our altars is most evident proof of that intense love for us with which his most Sacred Heart is filled. 4. Because, as our Blessed Lord nowhere meets with more neglect and insult than in this very sacrament of his love, so therefore, should the blessed eucharist be the special object towards which the members of the Confraternity of the Sacred Heart should direct their acts of reparation and atonement.

*Indulgences.*

Granted in perpetuity by the Sovereign Pontiffs, Pius VII., Leo XII., and Gregory XVI., to the members of the Pious Union of the Most Sacred Heart of Jesus, canonically erected in Rome, in the church of Sta. Maria *della Pace*, and which, by a brief dated

12th January, 1803, are extended to all other Confraternities of the Sacred Heart of Jesus, duly aggregated to the above.

1. Plenary, on the day of admisssion —(7th March, 1801). Usual conditions.

2. Plenary, on the Feast of Sacred Heart, or Sunday following. — (7th March, 1801,—12th July, 1803.) Usual conditions.

3. Plenary, on the first Friday or first Sunday of each month.—(15th July, 1803,—7th July, 1815.) Usual conditions.

4. Plenary, on one other day in each month.—(15th November, 1802.) Usual conditions.

5. Plenary, at the moment of death. —(7th March, 1801.)

6. Seven years and seven quarantines on each of the four Sundays preceding the Feast of the Sacred Heart.

7. Finally, an indulgence of sixty days for every pious work performed by members.—(7th March, 1801.)

Members, to be entitled to the foregoing indulgences, are required to recite habitually every day the prayers of the Confraternity, namely, the Lord's Prayer, Hail Mary, and Creed, with the aspiration, "Dearest Heart of Jesus, grant that I may love thee ever more and more."

By an Apostolic Brief, dated 2d April, 1805, the following additional indulgences have been granted in perpetuity to members of this Confraternity.

8. They who visit the church of the Confraternity on the days marked in the Roman Missal, and there pray according to the intentions of the Sovereign Pontiff, can gain the indulgences called those of the ROMAN STATIONS of which the following is a list:—

*Lent.*—An indulgence of 15 years and 15 quarantines on Ash Wednesday, and on the fourth Sunday. One of 25 years and 25 quarantines on Palm Sunday. Plenary on Holy Thursday. Usual conditions, besides the visit alluded to above. 30 years and

30 quarantines on Good Friday and on Holy Saturday. 10 years and 10 quarantines on every other day in Lent.

*Easter.*—Easter Day.—Plenary; same conditions as on Holy Thursday. 30 years and 30 quarantines on each day to Low Sunday, inclusively.

*Ascension.*—Plenary; same conditions as on Holy Thursday.

*Pentecost.*—10 years and 10 quarantines on the Vigil. 30 years and 30 quarantines on the Feast, and each day during the Octave to Saturday, inclusively.

*Advent.*—15 years and 15 quarantines on third Sunday.—10 years and 10 quarantines on each of the other Sundays.

*Christmas.*—15 years and 15 quarantines on Vigil; also, for assisting at midnight Mass, and the same for the Mass of the Aurora. Plenary on Feast; conditions as on Holy Thursday. 30 years and 30 quarantines on each of the three days immediately following Christmas, on the Circumcision, Epiphany, and also on each of the Sundays of Septuagesima, Sexagesima, and Quinquagesima.

*Quarter-Tense.*—On each quarter-tense day; 10 years and 10 quarantines.

*St. Mark's and Rogation days.*—30 years and 30 quarantines, each day.

9. Moreover, by a Brief, dated 2d April, 1805, a Plenary Indulgence is granted to Associates on the following feasts: Immaculate Conception, Nativity of the Blessed Virgin Mary, Annunciation, Purification, and Assumption; All Saints, Commemoration of All Souls, St. Joseph, SS. Peter and Paul, and St. John the Evangelist. The conditions for gaining these are, Confession, Communion, and a visit to a church of confraternity.

10. 7 years and 7 quarantines on the other Feasts of the Blessed Virgin and those of the other Apostles, on condition of visiting the church of the confraternity.

The indulgences under the numbers,

8, 9, and 10, to gain which a visit to the church or chapel of the confraternity is required, can still be gained by associates, who, from infirmity or other sufficient cause, are prevented from making the prescribed visit, on condition of their fulfilling some other pious work which can be enjoined, once for all, in its stead by their confessor.

11. An indulgence of seven years and seven quarantines may be gained on each day of the Novena or Triduo in preparation for the Feast of the Sacred Heart, by visiting devoutly a church or public oratory in which the Feast is celebrated, and praying there for some time according to the intentions of the Sovereign Pontiff (4th March, 1806; 21st May, 1828.)

12. A Plenary Indulgence is granted on each of the six Fridays or six Sundays immediately preceding the Feast of the Sacred Heart, to those who, having confessed and communicated, shall visit a church or oratory where the Feast is kept, and pray there as before

stated (4th March, 1806.) The **visit to** a church, prescribed for the Indulgences under numbers 11 and 12, can be commuted by their confessors into some other pious work in favor of those who are unable to make the visit.

All the indulgences granted to the Confraternity of the Sacred Heart can be gained by the faithful, in whatever part of the world they may be, where there does not exist a confraternity of the Sacred Heart, or where there is a difficulty of getting affiliated with the Arch-confraternity at Rome, provided always that they fulfil with exactitude the prescribed works (Pius VII, 15th May, 1816.)

13. Finally, a Plenary Indulgence is granted to associates on the Feast of St. Gregory the Great (March 12.) The conditions of which are, Confession, Communion, and visit to the church of the confraternity, with prayer offered for the Pope's intention (Gregory XVI., 20th June, 1834.) The

above indulgences are all applicable to the souls in Purgatory.

---

### Perpetual Adoration of the Sacred Heart.

Every member of the Society of the Sacred Heart may have himself enrolled for the Perpetual Adoration, which is intended as a means of procuring for this Adorable Heart a continual *cultus* or worship and expression of thanksgiving, in grateful recognition of the love for us with which this divine heart is filled. Those who enter themselves for the Perpetual Adoration are to make choice of some one or more days in the year; this day, or these days, they are to consecrate to the Sacred Heart of Jesus in the following manner. 1. They are to receive devoutly the sacraments of penance and the Blessed Eucharist. 2. They are to visit a church or public oratory, and there offer their prayers for the Sovereign Pontiff and all those in the sacred ministry, for the exaltation of the Church, for the extirpation of heresy, for the conversion of sinners, for peace and concord amongst Christian princes, for all those associated in this holy exercise, and for the holy souls in purgatory. 3. They are to renew their baptismal vows, as well as any others that they may at any time heretofore have made. 4. They are to make about one hour's prayer, either vocal or mental, at some time during the day. If, for some valid reason, this hour of prayer cannot be performed at one time, it is permitted to perform it at intervals during the day. 5. In order that this *cultus* may suitably represent that perpetual fire, which never shall go out on the altar (*Lev.* vi. 13), they are to offer up frequently during the day some ejaculatory prayer in honor of the Sacred Heart of Jesus. They who perform the above may gain on each occasion a Plenary Indulgence, applicable to the souls in Purgatory (Leo XI. 18th Feb., 1826; Greg. XVI., 20th June, 1834).

---

### Apostleship of Prayer.

The object of this Association is to induce Christians to take to heart the interests so dear to the Heart of Jesus, and to lead them to become as so many apostles for their promotion. This holy work of advancing the glory of God and extending the reign of his grace is to be accomplished by means of prayer. The spirit of this Association is precisely the same as that of the Confraternity of the Sacred Heart, with which, consequently, it is intimately connected.

All the indulgences granted to the Confraternity of the Sacred Heart may be gained by members of this Association, and, in addition, the following— *Plenary:* 1. On day of reception. 2. On the Feasts of the Sacred Heart of

Jesus and of the Immaculate Conception of the B. V. M. 3. On one Friday in each month, and also on one other day in the month at choice of members. The conditions for gaining these indulgences are, Confession, Communion, visit to a church, and prayer according to the Pope's intentions. Moreover, by a brief dated 21st Jan., 1850, all those who make each month a quarter of an hour's adoration before the Blessed Sacrament, endeavoring to appease the Divine Majesty, can gain a Plenary Indulgence on the following occasions: 1. On the day of the month assigned them for the performance of this devotion. 2. On Holy Thursday. 3. At the hour of death. Conditions as above.

An indulgence of 100 days is attached to the prayers and good works performed in accordance with the recommendations issued by the Director of the Association at the beginning of each month. Members are required to say, each day, the Lord's Prayer, Hail Mary, Creed, and the verse, "Dearest

Heart of Jesus, grant that I may love Thee daily more and more." All the above indulgences are applicable to the souls in Purgatory

---

## Statutes of the Pious Association of the Apostleship of Prayer.

*(Approved by the Sacred Congregation of Bishops, and Confirmed by the Sovereign Pontiff.)*

*Article* I. The Association of Prayer is neither a Sodality nor Confraternity in the strict sense of the term, but rather a kind of League of Prayer, in which not only the individual faithful, but still more, the pious Associations of believers, are invited to join. Hence, it is as little bound by the formalities requisite for the establishment of a Confraternity as the Association for the Propagation of the Faith, the object of which it serves to advance.

*Article* II. The sole condition imposed on the Associates of the Apostleship of Prayer, in order that they may share in the privileges granted to the Association by the Holy See, is that they should make all the intentions of the Most Sacred Heart of Jesus their own, *by offering up at least once a day, their daily prayers, works and trials,* for the end for which Christ our Lord ever prays and offers himself in sacrifice, especially for the Universal Church, for the Sovereign Pontiff, as well as for certain other urgent needs recommended each month by the General Director of the whole Association.

*Article* III. The Association of Prayer having been, by a Diploma dated 8th April, 1861, affiliated to the Arch-Confraternity of the S. Heart of Jesus, established at Rome in the Church *della Pace*, all the faithful who are members of the Association of Prayer, may, by that very fact, share in every indulgence and spiritual favor granted to the Arch-Confraternity aforesaid.

*Article* IV. Religious communities,

who may claim the foremost place in this league of prayer, are especially invited to enter into it, and even those may be admitted, whose rules preclude them from undertaking any additional duty, for the union of our intentions with those of the most Sacred Heart of Jesus, cannot be regarded as such. Religious communities, desirous of being affiliated, may obtain their wish *by enrolling the names of each of their members* in a Register drawn up by the Superior of each community, by the leave of the Director-General of the Apostleship, and sending an accurate copy of the same, that it may be entered in the General Register. The Superior of the community will give to each one a ticket of affiliation.

*Article* V. Religious communities, hospitals, boarding schools of religious, even whole parishes, may be affiliated in the manner aforesaid. But each member of these several Associations must be enrolled on a particular Register, and receive a ticket of affiliation from the Superior or Parish Priest, or any other person appointed thereto by the Director-General or any Central Director. Nor shall any one be held to have ceased to belong to the Association in consequence of having left any of these Associations of which he was a member.

*Article* VI. Those of the faithful who are not members of any Confraternity or Association affiliated to the Association of Prayer, may be admitted into it by having their names entered on the Registers kept by these several communities or associations already affiliated, and receiving a ticket of admission. It is left to each person to appoint the day of his admission, whereon he may gain the Plenary Indulgence attached thereto.

*Article* VII. The General-Director of the Association may not only issue diplomas of affiliation, but may further empower Local Directors to issue the same in his name in a determinate number.

*Article* VIII. In every country where the Apostleship of Prayer is, or shall hereafter be, established, it shall be lawful for the General-Director to appoint Central Directors, who may give diplomas of affiliation to communities, parishes, and other associations, and though the names have to be sent up to the General-Director, their admission shall be held to date from the day whereon they have received their diploma from the Central Director.

*Article* IX. In no diocese shall the Apostleship be established, but with the consent of the local Ordinary, whose jurisdiction over the associates living in his diocese must remain untouched, according to the tenor of the Sacred Canons and Apostolic Constitutions.

At an audience granted to the Secretary of the Sacred Congregation of Bishops and Regulars, on the 27th July, 1866, His Holiness approved and confirmed the statutes set forth above.

At a further audience on 24th May,

1867, the Holy Father granted the petition of the Bishop of Puy, and has commanded that the Statutes be so far amended that the Local Directors be not bound to send to the General-Director their lists of associates, and that the giving of tickets of admission be dispensed with in those cases only in which it is impossible to give them, and lastly, that the General-Director of this pious Union be one of the Fathers of the Society of Jesus, to be appointed by the General of said Society, for the time being.

## Litany of the Saints.

*This is the only litany which forms part of the regular and appointed offices of the Church, and is used on occasions of public humiliation, etc.*

Remember not, O Lord, our offences, nor those of our fathers; neither take thou vengeance of our sins.

Lord, have mercy on us.
*Lord, have mercy on us.*
Christ, have mercy on us.
*Christ, have mercy on us,*
Lord, have mercy on us.
*Lord, have mercy on us.*
Christ, hear us,
*Christ, graciously hear us.*
God, the Father of heaven,
 *Have mercy on us,*
God the Son, Redeemer of the world,
 *Have mercy on us,*
God the Holy Ghost,
 *Have mercy on us,*
Holy Trinity, one God,
 *Have mercy on us,*
Holy Mary, *Pray for us.*
Holy Mother of God, *Pray for us.*
Holy Virgin of virgins, *Pray for us.*

St. Michael,
St. Gabriel,
St. Raphael,
All ye holy angels and archangels,
All ye holy Orders of blessed spirits,
St. John Baptist,
St. Joseph,
All ye holy patriarchs and prophets,
St. Peter,
St. Paul,
St. Andrew,
St. James,
St. John,
St. Thomas,
St. James,
St. Philip,
St. Bartholomew,
St. Matthew,
St. Simon,
St. Thaddeus,
St. Matthias,
St. Barnabas,
St. Luke,
St. Mark,
All ye holy apostles and evangelists,
All ye holy disciples of our Lord,

*Pray for us.*

## LITANY OF THE SAINTS.

All ye holy innocents,
St. Stephen,
St. Lawrence,
St. Vincent.
SS. Fabian and Sebastian,
SS. John and Paul,
SS. Cosmas and Damian,
SS. Gervase and Protase,
All ye holy martyrs,
St. Sylvester,
St. Gregory,
St. Ambrose,
St. Augustine,
St. Jerome,
St. Martin,
St. Nicholas,
All ye holy bishops and confessors,
All ye holy doctors,
St. Anthony,
St. Benedict,
St. Bernard,
St. Dominic,
St. Francis,
All ye holy priests and levites,
All ye holy monks and hermits,
St. Mary Magdalene,

} *Pray for us.*

St. Agatha,
St. Lucy,
St. Agnes,
St. Cecilia,
St. Catharine,
St. Anastasia,
All ye holy virgins and widows,
} *Pray for us.*

All ye holy men and women, saints of God,
*Make intercession for us,*
Be merciful,
*Spare us, O Lord,*
Be merciful,
*Graciously hear us, O Lord.*

From all evil,
From all sin,
From thy wrath,
From sudden and unprovided death,
From the snares of the devil,
From anger, and hatred, and all ill-will,
From the spirit of fornication,
From lightning and tempest,
From everlasting death,
Through the mystery of thy holy incarnation,
} *O Lord, deliver us.*

## LITANY OF THE SAINTS.

Through thy coming,
Through thy nativity,
Through thy baptism and holy fasting,
Through thy cross and passion,
Through thy death and burial,
Through thy holy resurrection,
Through thy admirable ascension,
Through the coming of the Holy Ghost, the Paraclete,
In the day of judgment.

*O Lord, deliver us.*

We sinners, *Beseech thee, hear us.*

That thou wouldst spare us,
That thou wouldst pardon us,
That thou wouldst bring us to true penance,
That thou wouldst vouchsafe to govern and preserve thy holy Church,
That thou wouldst vouchsafe to preserve our Apostolic Prelate, and all Orders of the Church in holy religion,
That thou wouldst vouchsafe to humble the enemies of holy Church,

*We beseech thee, hear us.*

## LITANY OF THE SAINTS.

That thou wouldst vouchsafe to give peace and true concord to Christian kings and princes,

That thou wouldst vouchsafe to grant peace and unity to all Christian people,

That thou wouldst vouchsafe to confirm and preserve us in thy holy service,

That thou wouldst lift up our minds to heavenly desires,

That thou wouldst render eternal blessings to all our benefactors,

That thou wouldst deliver our souls, and the souls of our brethren, relations, and benefactors, from eternal damnation,

That thou wouldst vouchsafe to give and preserve the fruits of the earth,

That thou wouldst vouchsafe to grant eternal rest to all the faithful departed,

That thou wouldst vouchsafe graciously to hear us,

*We beseech thee, hear us.*

Son of God, *We beseech thee, etc.*
Lamb of God, who takest away the sins of the world,
*Spare us, O Lord.*
Lamb of God, who takest away the sins of the world,
*Graciously hear us, O Lord.*
Lamb of God, who takest away the sins of the world,
*Have mercy on us.*
Christ, hear us.
*Christ, graciously hear us.*
Lord, have mercy on us.
*Christ, have mercy on us.*
Lord, have mercy on us.

Our Father (*secretly*),
And lead us not into temptation.
R. But deliver us from evil.

O God, come to my assistance; O Lord, make haste to help me.

Let them be confounded and ashamed that seek my soul.

Let them be turned backward and blush for shame that desire evils to me.

Let them be presently turned away

blushing for shame that say unto me: 'Tis well, 'tis well.

Let all that seek thee rejoice and be glad in thee; and let such as love thy salvation say always: The Lord be magnified.

But I am needy and poor, O God, help me.

Thou art my helper and my deliverer: O Lord, make no delay.

Glory be, etc.

Save thy servants.

*R.* Who hope in thee, O my God.

Be unto us, O Lord, a tower of strength.

*R.* From the face of the enemy.

Let not the enemy prevail against us.

*R.* Nor the son of iniquity approach to hurt us.

O Lord, deal not with us according to our sins.

*R.* Neither requite us according to our iniquities.

Let us pray for our Sovereign Pontiff, N.

*R.* The Lord preserve him and give

him life, and make him blessed upon the earth; and deliver him not up to the will of his enemies.

Let us pray for our benefactors.

R. Vouchsafe, O Lord, for thy name's sake to reward with eternal life all them that do us good. Amen.

Let us pray for the faithful departed.

R. Eternal rest give unto them, O Lord: and let perpetual light shine upon them.

Let them rest in peace.

R. Amen.

For our absent brethren.

R. Save thy servants, who hope in thee, O my God.

Send them help, O Lord, from thy holy place.

R. And defend them out of Sion.

O Lord, hear my prayer.

R. And let my cry come unto thee.

### LET US PRAY.

O God, whose property is always to have mercy and to spare, receive our humble petition; that we, and all thy servants who are bound by the chain of sins, may, by the compassion of thy goodness, mercifully be absolved.

Graciously hear, we beseech thee, O Lord, the prayers of thy suppliants, and forgive the sins of them that confess to thee; that, in thy bounty, thou mayest grant us both pardon and peace.

Show forth upon us, O Lord, in thy mercy, thy unspeakable loving-kindness; that thou mayest both loose us from all our sins, and deliver us from the punishment which we deserve for them.

O God, who by sin art offended, and by penance pacified, mercifully regard the prayers of thy people making supplication to thee, and turn away the scourges of thine anger, which we deserve for our sins.

Almighty, everlasting God, have mercy upon thy servant, N., our Sovereign Pontiff, and direct him, according to thy clemency, into the way of everlasting salvation; that by thy grace he may both desire those things that are pleasing to thee, and perform them with all his strength.

O God, from whom all holy desires, all right counsels, and all just works, do come, give unto thy servants that peace which the world cannot give; that both our hearts being devoted to the keeping of thy commandments, and the fear of enemies being taken away, the times may, by thy protection, be peaceful.

Inflame, O Lord, our reins and hearts with the fire of the Holy Ghost; that we may serve thee with a chaste body, and please thee with a clean heart.

O God, the Creator and Redeemer of all the faithful, give to the souls of thy servants departed the remission of all their sins; that through pious supplications they may obtain the pardon which they have always desired.

Prompt, we beseech thee, O Lord, our actions by thy inspirations, and further them by thy continual help; that every prayer and work of ours may always begin from thee, and through thee be likewise ended.

Almighty, everlasting God, who hast dominion over the living and the dead, and art merciful to all whom thou foreknowest will be thine by faith and works; we humbly beseech thee that they for whom we intend to pour forth our prayers, whether this present world still retains them in the flesh, or the world to come hath already received them stripped of their mortal bodies, may, by the grace of thy loving-kindness, and by the intercession of all the saints, obtain the remission of all their sins. R. Amen.

O Lord, hear my prayer. R. And let my cry come unto thee. May the Almighty, etc. R. Amen.

And may the souls, etc. Amen.

## Prayers to the Most Holy Wounds.

### AN ACT OF CONTRITION.

As I kneel before thee on the cross, most loving Saviour of my soul, my conscience reproaches me with having nailed thee to that cross with these hands of mine, as often as I have fallen into mortal sin, wearying thee with my monstrous ingratitude. My God, my chief and most perfect good, worthy of all my love, because thou hast ever loaded me with blessings, I cannot now undo my misdeeds, as I would most willingly; but I will loathe them, grieving greatly for having offended thee, who art infinite goodness. And now, kneeling at thy feet, I will try, at least, to compassionate thee, to give thee thanks, to ask of thee pardon and contrition; wherefore, with heart and lips, I say:

### TO THE FIRST WOUND, OF THE LEFT FOOT.

Holy wound of the left foot of my Jesus, I adore thee; I compassionate thee for the most bitter pain which thou didst suffer. I thank thee for the love whereby thou wast wearied in overtaking me on the way to ruin, and didst bleed amid the thorns and brambles of my sins. I offer to the Eternal Father the pain and love of thy most holy humanity, in atonement for my sins, all which I detest with sincere and bitter contrition.

(*Our Father, Hail Mary, Glory, etc.*)

Holy Mother, pierce me through,
In my heart each wound renew
Of my Saviour crucified.

### TO THE SECOND WOUND, OF THE RIGHT FOOT.

Holy wound of the right foot of my

Jesus, I adore thee; I compassionate thee for the bitter pain which thou didst suffer. I thank thee for that love which pierced thee with such torture and shedding of blood, in order to punish my wanderings and the guilty pleasures I have granted to my unbridled passion. I offer the Eternal Father all the pain and love of thy most holy humanity, and I pray unto you for grace to weep over my transgressions with burning tears, and to enable me to persevere in the good which I have begun, without ever swerving again from my obedience to the commandments of my God.

(*Our Father, Hail Mary, Glory, etc.*
(*Holy Mother, etc.*)

### TO THE THIRD WOUND, OF THE LEFT HAND.

Holy wound of the left hand of my

Jesus, I adore thee; I compassionate thee for the bitter pain which thou didst suffer. I thank thee for having, in thy love, spared me the scourges and eternal damnation which my sins had merited. I offer to the Eternal Father the pain and love of thy most holy humanity; and I pray thee to teach me how to turn to good account my span of life, and bring forth in it worthy fruits of penance, and so disarm the justice of God, which I have provoked.

(*Our Father, Hail Mary, Glory, etc.*)
(*Holy Mother, etc.*)

### TO THE FOURTH WOUND, OF THE RIGHT HAND.

Holy wound of the right hand of my Jesus, I adore thee; I compassionate thee for the bitter pain which thou didst suffer. I thank thee for thy grace lavished on me with such love, in spite of all my most perverse obstinacy. I offer to the Eternal Father all the pain and love of thy most holy humanity; and I pray thee to change my heart and its affections, and make me do all my actions in accordance with the will of God.

(*Our Father, Hail Mary, Glory, etc.*)
(*Holy Mother, etc.*)

### TO THE FIFTH WOUND, OF THE SACRED SIDE.

Holy wound in the side of my Jesus, I adore thee; I compassionate thee for the cruel insult thou didst suffer. I thank thee, my Jesus, for the love which suffered thy side and Heart to be pierced, that so the last drops of blood and water might issue forth, making my redemption to abound. I offer to the Eternal Father this outrage, and the love of thy most holy humanity, that my soul may enter once for all into that most loving Heart, eager and ready to receive the greatest sinners, and never more depart.

*(Our Father, Hail Mary, Glory, etc.)*
*(Holy Mother, etc.)*

# THY KINGDOM COME.

## APOSTLESHIP OF PRAYER

### The Holy League

#### OF THE

# Sacred Heart of Jesus.

### Certificate ✠ of ✠ Admission

*Edward Sheridan,*

has been enrolled in the APOSTLESHIP OF PRAYER, the Holy League of the SACRED HEART OF JESUS, this *12th* day of *June* in the year of our Lord 18*94*.

EMILE REGNAULT, S.J.,
*Director-General.*

## The Morning Offering.

O Jesus, through the Immaculate Heart of Mary, I offer Thee the prayers, work, and sufferings of this day for all the intentions of Thy Divine Heart, in union with the Holy Sacrifice of the Mass.

**The Apostleship of Prayer** is a League for spreading devotion to the Sacred Heart.

**Its special objects** are to promote what the Sacred Heart is ever pleading for in the Tabernacle and on the Altar, the salvation of souls and the triumph of the Church; and to make reparation for sin.

**The one duty** is simple and easy for all. It is to offer in the morning, the prayers, actions, and sufferings of the day, for the intentions of the Sacred Heart. This may be done in any words, or even in thought only. (See short form on preceding page.)

**The advantages** are very great, both to ourselves and others:

1. It is a special title to the love of the Sacred Heart. "Those," our Lord says, "who promote this devotion shall have their names written in My Heart, never to be blotted out."

2. The merit of each action of the day is increased.

3. Every action becomes a new aid to the Church, a new shield lifted against her enemies, a new help to souls perishing on earth, and suffering in Purgatory.

4. We are prayed for, daily, by millions of fellow members, including an immense number of holy religious.

5. We share in the merits of all the Religious Orders: the Benedictines, Carthusians, Trappists, Carmelites, Franciscans, Poor Clares, Dominicans, Augustinians, Jesuits, Redemptorists, Marists, Lazarists, Sisters of Charity, and many others, have all granted this favor to the League; and their Masses, Holy Communions, and good works will plead for us after death.

6. Moreover, there are very large Indulgences (of which the principal are noted on the next page).

7. Its happy results soon show themselves in parishes, not only in a more loving spirit of devotion, but in the better and more frequent use of the Sacraments.

## Principal Indulgences.

*(All are applicable to the souls in Purgatory. The conditions, common to all, are Confession, Communion, and visit to a church with prayer for the intentions of the Holy Father.)*

**I.** All who make the *Morning Offering* can gain:

1. A Plenary Indulgence on the day of admission, the feast of the Sacred Heart (or Sunday following), the Immaculate Conception, and one Friday and one other day in each month (for this last, Communion alone suffices). Also, on the day appointed every month for the General Communion of Reparation.

Also, during night from Thursday to Friday of each week, or at common hour appointed by Local Director, for the practice of the *Holy Hour*.

Also, for Communion on Patron Saint's day assigned on *Monthly Rosary Ticket*.

Also, for a second Communion at Easter-time in reparation for Christians who neglect their duty.

**2. An Indulgence of 100 days for each action offered for the intentions of the Apostleship.**

**3. An Indulgence of 100 days each time that an Associate, wearing the Badge of the Apostleship, repeats, orally or mentally, the aspiration—"Thy Kingdom Come." Also, 7 years and 7 quarantines, if worn visibly before Blessed Sacrament exposed.**

**II.** All who to the daily offering of actions add the daily recitation of a *decade of the Rosary* can gain:

1. Plenary Indulgences on the feasts of the Prayer in the Garden, the Most Pure Heart of Mary, and the Patronage of St. Joseph.

2. An Indulgence of 100 days each time.

3. If beads bearing the *Apostolic Indulgences* are used, and *one day* each week five decades (*the entire beads*) are said, a Plenary Indulgence on Christmas Day, the Epiphany, Easter Sunday, the Ascension, Pentecost, Trinity Sunday, Corpus Christi, the Assumption and Nativity of the Blessed Virgin, the Nativity of St. John the Baptist, the feasts of St. Joseph, of the Apostles (St. Matthias included), the feast of All Saints, and at the hour of death.

4. If beads bearing the *Indulgences of St. Bridget* are used, a Plenary Indulgence on the feast of St. Bridget (Oct. 8), and at the hour of death, and an Indulgence of 100 days attached to each bead of the Rosary.

N. B.—Directors of the Apostleship who have fifty Associates reciting the daily decade have the faculty of attaching to the beads the Apostolic and Bridgettine Indulgences, provided a monthly meeting of the League be held in the church.

**III.** All who practise the *Communion of Reparation* gain a Plenary Indulgence each time, and at the hour of death; also the day when they are entered on a weekly or monthly list.

**IV.** *Twenty-six* Special Plenary Indulgences for *Promoters* who have received Diploma and Cross from Central Director.

(The days of Plenary Indulgence are noted in Calendar of *Messenger* and on monthly *Rosary Ticket*.)

## INDULGENCED PRAYERS.
*(From Authentic Rescripts.)*

Sweet Heart of my Jesus, make me love Thee ever more and more. (*300 days, Plenary once a month, if said daily.*)

Jesus, meek and humble of Heart, make my heart like unto Thine. (*300 days.*)

Sweet Heart of Jesus, be my love!
Sweet Heart of Mary, be my salvation!
(*300 days each; Plenary once a month, if said daily.*)

*Imprimatur*—
　　† PATRITIUS J.,
　　　*Archiepiscopus Philadelphiensis.*

---

*For their intelligent devotion, and for a knowledge of the intentions recommended to their prayers each month the Associates are referred to the publications of the Apostleship of Prayer*—**Messenger** *and* **Decade Leaflets.** *These, with Handbook, Certificates, Badges, etc., should be procured from the Central Director, who also gives diplomas establishing new Centres of the League.*

**Address**
　　　APOSTLESHIP OF PRAYER,
　　　　　1611 Girard Avenue,
　　　　　　　Philadelphia, Pa.

## Practices of the Apostleship of Prayer.

### 1st Degree: THE MORNING OFFERING.

O Jesus, through the Immaculate Heart of Mary, I offer Thee the prayers, work and sufferings of this day for all the intentions of Thy Divine Heart, in union with the Holy Sacrifice of the Mass; and in particular for *the Churches of the East.*

### 2d Degree: THE ROSARY DECADE.

2D SORROWFUL MYSTERY—THE SCOURGING.

Lord, grant the protection of Thy Divine Heart to our Holy Father, the Pope.

### 3d Degree: COMMUNION OF REPARATION.

*General*, if not designated, *Sunday, Sept. 16th.
*Perpetual*, *monthly bands . . *weekly . . . . . . .
*Individual*, if not designated, *Sept. . .   or feast of
YOUR PATRON: *St. Thomas of Villanova, Sept. 22d.
HOLY HOUR, in common, *Sept.      . . .
*Fruit:* **Patience.**—Whosoever doth not carry his cross and come after me, cannot be my disciple.
*Luke xiv. 27.*

*Plenary Indulgence for Associates of League.*

## *September General Intention, 1894.*

Specially blessed by His Holiness Leo XIII.

### The Churches of the East.

*100 days' Indulgence for each action offered for these Intentions of our Associates in the United States.*

1. S. St. Giles, Abbot.—Directors' Intentions.
2. S. St. Stephen, King.—28,406 Thanksgivings.
3. M. Sts. Seraphia, Sabina, MM.-16,863 in Affliction.
4. T. St. Rose, Viterbo, V.—17,404 Dead Associates.
5. W. St. Lawrence Justinian, Bp.—50,318 Special.
6. Th. St. Onesiphorus, M.—6,880 Communities.
7. \*F St. Regina, V. M.—23,162 First Communions.
8. S. Nativity of B. V. M.—59,580 Departed Souls.
9. S. St. P. Claver, C.—32,651 Employment, means.
10. M. St. Nicholas of Tolentino.—23,331 Clergy.
11. T. Bl. C. Spinola and Comp., MM.—84,442 Children.
12. W. St. Guy, C.—33,642 Families.
13. Th St. Frederick, C.—86,762 Perseverance.
14. F. Exaltation of Holy Cross.-8,232 Reconciliations.
15. †S. St. Catharine, Genoa, W.—41,464 Spir. Favors.
16. \*S. Seven Sorrows, B. V. M.—24,330 Temp. Favors.
17. M. Stigmata of St. Fr. of Assisi.-28,486 Conversions.
18. T. St. Joseph, Cupertino.—30,426 Young Persons.
19. W. Sts. Januarius and Comp., MM.—19,781 Schools.
20. Th. Sts. Eustace and Comp., MM.—18,623 Sick.
21. F. St. Matthew, Ap.—5,195 Missions and Retreats.
22. S. St. Thomas of Villanova.—11,365 Societies.
23. S. St. Thecla, V. M.—58,771 Sinners.
24. M. Our Lady of Mercy.—19,394 Parents.
25. T. St. Cleophas.—68,640 Religious.
26. W Sts. Cyprian, Justina, MM.—23,867 Novices.
27. Th. Sts. Cosmas and Damian, MM.—9,417 Superiors.
28. F. St. Wenceslas, M.—13,856 Vocations.
29. †S. St. Michael, Archangel.—11,320 Promoters.
30. S. St. Jerome, D.—Messenger Readers.

(\**Plenary Indulgence for Associates;* †*for Promoters.*)

*Recommend also Intentions of Associates throughout the world.*

After September 15, 1894, all communications for the Apostleship of Prayer, League of the Sacred Heart, or for the Messenger of the Sacred Heart and Pilgrim of Our Lady of Martyrs, should be addressed

APOSTLESHIP OF PRAYER,
27 and 29 West Sixteenth Street,
New York City, N Y

## Practices of the Apostleship of Prayer.

### 1st Degree: THE MORNING OFFERING.

O Jesus, through the Immaculate Heart of Mary, I offer Thee the prayers, work, and sufferings of this day for all the intentions of Thy Divine Heart, in union with the Holy Sacrifice of the Mass; and in particular for *the Devotion to the Holy Angels.*

### 2d Degree: THE ROSARY DECADE.

5TH JOYFUL MYSTERY—FINDING IN THE TEMPLE.

Lord, grant the protection of Thy Divine Heart to our Holy Father, the Pope.

### 3d Degree: COMMUNION OF REPARATION.

*General,* if not designated, \*Sunday, Oct. 21st.
*Perpetual,* \*monthly bands . . \*weekly . .
*Individual,* if not designated, \*Oct. . or feast of
YOUR PATRON: \*St. Luke, Evangelist, Oct. 18th.
HOLY HOUR, in common, \*Oct. .
*Fruit:* **Love of Holy Communion.**—A soul can do nothing more pleasing to God than to receive Him frequently in the Sacrament of the Altar.
*St. Alph. Liguori*

\**Plenary Indulgence for Associates of League.*

## October General Intention, 1894.

Specially blessed by His Holiness Leo XIII.

### Devotion to the Holy Angels.

*Intentions of our Associates in the United States.*

1. M. St. Remigius, Bp.—Directors' Intentions.
2. T Holy Guardian Angels—162,866 Thanksgivings.
3. W. St Thomas, Bp. 58,321 in affliction.
4. †Th St. Francis of Assisi, F. (O.S.F.)—68,534 Dead Associates.
5. *F. SS. Placidus, Comp., MM.—228,353 Special.
6. S. St. Bruno, F. (Carth.).—34,232 Communities.
7. S. Most Holy Rosary.—60,569 First Communions.
8. M. St. Bridget, W.—338,995 Departed Souls.
9. T. SS. Denis and Companions, MM.—119,104 Employment, means.
10. W. St. Francis Borgia, (S.J.)—89 935 Clergy.
11. Th. Bl. John Leonard.—328,298 Children.
12. F. St. Wilfred, Bp.—102,897 Families.
13. S. St. Edward, (King).—191,136 Perseverance.
14. S. Maternity B.V.M.—40,701 Reconciliations.
15. †M. St. Teresa, V. (O.D.C.)—156,539 Spiritual Favors.
16. T. St. Coleman, Bp.—108 947 Temporal Favors.
17. W. St. Hedwige, W., Bl. Margaret Mary, (see 25th).—108,781 Conversions
18. Th. St. Luke, Evang.—152,789 Young Persons.
19. F St. Peter of Alcantara (O.S.F.) 42.433 Schools.
20. S. St. John Cantius (Parish Priest).—84,430 Sick.
21. *S. Purity B.V.M.—31,163 Missions, Retreats.
22. M. St. Mary Salome.—26,808 Spiritual Works, Societies.
23. T. The Most Holy Redeemer.—230,930 Sinners.
24. W. St. Raphael, Archangel.—149,050 Parents-
25. Th. Bl. Margaret Mary.—245,333 Religious
26. F. The Holy Relics.—66,558 Seminarists, Novices.
27. S. St. Ives, (Lawyer).—37,689 Parishes.
28. S. SS. Simon and Jude, Apostles.—38,022 Superiors.
29. M. Venerable Bede, D.—51,101 Vocations.
30. T. St. Alphonsus S.J—64,547 Promoters.
31. W. St. Quentin, M.—Messenger Readers.

*Recommend also Intentions of Associates throughout the world.*

(*Plenary Indulgence for Associates ; †for Promoters.)

Directors or Secretaries of Centres should summarize and send Intentions to the Apostleship of Prayer, 27 and 29 W. 16th St., New York, so as to have them recorded before the first of each month. They are published in the *Calendars* and *Pilgrim*, forwarded to the Director-General, who has Mass said for them daily at the General Direction Toulouse, and then has them placed on the altar at Lourdes.

www.ingramcontent.com/pod-product-compliance
Lightning Source LLC
Chambersburg PA
CBHW032224230426
43666CB00033B/1207